ISLAM AND RELIGIOUS PLURALISM

ISLAM AND RELIGIOUS PLURALISM

Āyatullāh Murtaḍhā Muṭahharī

Translated by Sayyid Sulayman Ali Hasan
Introduction by Sayyid Muhammad Rizvi
Foreword by Hasnain Walji

TABLE OF CONTENTS

FOREWORD i

INTRODUCTION v

BIOGRAPHY OF THE AUTHOR xxi

GOOD DEEDS OF NON MUSLIMS 27

Outline of the Discussion 27
1. The General Aspect of the Discussion 30
2. No Religion Except al-Islam is Accepted 32

Good Deeds Without Faith 35
Two Ways of Thinking 36
The Third Logic 37
The So-Called Intellectuals 37
The Rigid Group 41

Value of Belief 44
1. Being Held Accountable For Unbelief 45
Levels of Submission 45
True Islam and Regional Islam 48
2. Sincerity, the Condition for the Acceptance of Actions 50
Quality or Quantity? 56
The Mosque of Bahlūl 58
3. Belief in God and the Hereafter 59
Belief in the Prophecy and Imāmate 65
4. Affliction 68

Below the Zero Point 74
The Incapable and the Powerless 75
From the View of the Islamic Sages 82

The Sins of Muslims 85
Creational Conditions and Conventional Conditions 90

Summary and Conclusion 95

بسم الله الرحمن الرحيم

In the Name of God, the Most Gracious, the Most Merciful

FOREWORD

Where will Mother Teresa go ?

Some years ago, in Brampton, Ontario, Canada, one of my lectures on the subject of religious pluralism provoked the question: 'Where will Mother Teresa go – Heaven or Hell?' This was in reaction to my submission challenging the notion of religious pluralism, reflecting on discussions within the academia that "all roads lead to Rome."

My subsequent deliberations with a number of young intellectuals in the audience quickly revealed their unawareness that the original concept of religious pluralism was a subtle defence to the doctrine of salvation through Christ; thereby, providing in Christianity, toleration for other religions.

Essentially, the roots of religious pluralism lie in the development of political liberalism in eighteenth century Europe, which was heeling from the horrible tales of religious persecution. The Enlightened European thinkers of the time were reacting to religious intolerance, which had resulted in the history of sectarian wars to be avoided by all means. Having witnessed the consequences of religious intolerance, the eighteenth century European Christians were anxious to recover through an ideology that was entrenched in religious principles and thereby securing its permanent effect of ensuring peace and progress in Europe - both politically and philosophically - whilst preserving the sanctity of Christianity.

The principal advocate, Professor John Hick, devised the original concept of religious pluralism by incorporating the Christian doctrine of salvation, allowing almost anyone to enter heaven.

Ironically to make his case, Hick used, amongst other arguments, Rumi's fable of the blind men describing an elephant thus, suggesting that in our visualization of the ultimate reality, we are in the position of the blind men describing the elephant. Our ultimate reality is limited by the structures of the various religions. In other words, be it through the trunk, leg or the ear, it was sufficient to conceptualize the elephant! Paradoxically, Rumi used the parable to demonstrate our limitations in knowing the ultimate reality. Hick expounded religious pluralism by suggesting that the world's numerous faiths had reconcilable differences in striving for the ultimate reality.

It is indeed a sorry state of affairs that when we are blessed with far more profound answers to the issues of rigid exclusivity offered by Islam that Muslim intellectuals should be impressed by Hick's weak defence on the subject. Hence, to enable us to better understand the Islamic perspective on religious pluralism, this translation of the Persian essay on *Islam and Religious Pluralism* by Ayatullāh Mutahhari is very timely. Indeed the first edition of this publication proved to be so popular, that a second revised edition - the book you now have on your hands - has been published.

This work is yet another example of the scholar's inspired foresight as decades ago, he undertook to address the topical questions which vex Muslim youths exposed to Western academia today!

It is important to mention that this essay is part of a compilation on the broader subject of *Divine Justice* by the author. That he has chosen to address the issue of religious pluralism under the heading of Divine Justice is a telling enunciation of the fundamental belief in the justice of God – that no good act will go unrewarded. Thus, this book offers rational answers to questions such as: will the great inventors and scientists, despite their worthy services for humanity, go to Hell? Will the likes of Pasteur and Edison go to Hell whilst indolent people who have spent their lives in a corner of the mosque go to Heaven? Has God created Heaven solely for a given minority?

In contrast to Hick's compromising view, Shi'a scholars generally agree that God's damnation does not arbitrarily apply to all who lack faith in His revelations. For instance, exceptions are made for those who are incapable *(qāṣir)* such as children and adults who are intellectually impaired. Uniquely, most Shi'a scholars make a distinction between the incapable and the negligent *(muqaṣṣir)* who have misplaced convictions despite having access to Islam.

The late Ayatullāh Mutahhari's enquiry into the problem of religious pluralism elaborated the distinction of these two categories.

What is even more interesting, however, is that he defines the category of the incapable to include those for whom Islam has not been accessible! For instance, remote residences where Islam has not been propagated or those living in an Islamaphobic environment which has resulted in ill-founded misconceptions!

Ayatullāh Mutahhari's brilliant rationale of the incapable clearly establishes that heaven has not been reserved for a minority within a minority, thus, boldly answering the dogmatism actively promoted by those he has identified in his essay as *"narrow minded dry holy ones."*

This facet has another important consideration. In this day and age when Islam is mis-defined by fanatical elements within the Muslim community, and such misperception are fanned by the media under in the name of freedom of speech, issues addressed in this book; invite us towards greater understanding and peaceful co-existence, especially amongst all people of faith.

Hasnain Walji
Plano, Texas
March 8th 2006

INTRODUCTION

Is Islam the only right path? Is as-Ṣirātul Mustaqīm (the right path) a single phenomena or are there multiple paths leading to the same destination? What happens to the non-Muslims who live a decent life and do not violate the rights of other people? Do they gain salvation, and go to Paradise or not? These are some of the burning questions of the modern era.

The concept of religious pluralism is not new; it has been discussed in one form or another by past philosophers and theologians of various schools. However, with the increased interaction between followers of different religions and inter-faith dialogues, religious pluralism has taken a new life in the stream of current thought.

When the great philosopher, Āyatullāh Murtaḍhā Muṭahharī, wrote his seminal work, *'Adl-e Ilāhī* (The Divine Justice) about thirty-five years ago, the debate on religious pluralism had not yet become that popular in Iran. What you have in your hands is the translation of *The Divine Justice's* last chapter on "Good Deeds of Non-Muslims". The more appropriate place to discuss religious pluralism and its related issues would be under the theme of "prophethood" when discussing the finality of Prophet Muḥammad's prophethood, however the question "What happens to the good deeds of non-Muslims?" is also connected to the theme of Divine justice; and so Āyatullāh Muṭahharī has answered it at the end of his work, *The Divine Justice.*

Nonetheless, before discussing that question in detail, Āyatullāh Muṭahharī has also briefly stated his views on religious pluralism itself. As you will read yourself, he expresses the prevailing view of the Muslim theologians and philosophers that Islam is the only right path. However, and more importantly, he cautions the readers not to jump to the conclusion that since Islam is the only right path therefore all non-Muslims will go to hell. The exclusivist view of

Islam being the right path does not automatically and necessarily lead to the belief that all non-Muslims will go to hell.

In the last one and a half decades, the question of religious pluralism has been passionately debated among the Muslims in the West as well as the East. Some Muslim intellectuals have even tried to impose the concept of religious pluralism onto the Qur'an itself!

I would like to take this opportunity to briefly present this discussion as a preamble to the writing of the great scholar, Āyatullāh Murtaḍhā Muṭahharī.

While discussing the concept of pluralism in the Islamic context, it is important to define the term clearly. Pluralism can be used in two different meanings: "Social pluralism" in the sociological sense means a society which consists of a multi-faith or multi-cultural mosaic. "Religious pluralism" in the theological sense means a concept in which all religions are considered to be equally true and valid.

Social Pluralism

As far as social pluralism is concerned, Islam seeks for peaceful co-existence and mutual tolerance between the people of different religions and cultures. Among the three Abrahamic religions, it is only Islam which has accorded recognition to Judaism and Christianity. Judaism does not recognize Jesus as the awaited Messiah or the Prophet; and Christianity does not recognize Muḥammad as the true Prophet and Messenger of God.

In the Islamic worldview, God sent many prophets and messengers to guide mankind; the number given in the traditions is 124,000 prophets. The first prophet was Ādam and the last Prophet was Muḥammad - the Prophet of Islam. However, not all the 124,000 prophets were of the same rank and status.[1] Five of these prophets are given the highest rank in the spiritual hierarchy: and they are Noah, Abraham, Moses, Jesus, and Muḥammad. Almighty Allāh says in the Qur'an: *"And when We made a covenant with the prophets: with you, with Noah, Abraham, Moses, and Jesus, son of Mary ..."*[2]

A Muslim is required to believe in all the prophets, otherwise he cannot be considered a "Muslim".[3] If a person, for instance, says that I believe in Muḥammad, Jesus, Abraham, Noah but not in Moses as one of the prophets of God, then he cannot be accepted as a Muslim; similarly, if a person believes in all the prophets but refuses to accept Jesus as one of the prophets and messengers of God, then he is not a Muslim. That is why Islam considers the Christian and the Jewish communities as "the People of the Book" or "the People of Scripture" (*Ahlul Kitāb*). Islam has even allowed a Muslim man to marry a Christian or Jewish woman, but not those from the other faiths.

What is noteworthy is that Islam accorded this recognition to the People of the Book fourteen centuries ago when there was absolutely no talk of tolerance among people of different faiths or an ecumenical movement among religions.[4]

On a socio-political level, a Muslim government would readily sign an agreement with its Christian and Jewish minorities. Imām 'Alī Zaīnul 'Ābidīn[5], the great-grandson of the Prophet, writes: *"It is the right of the non-Muslims living in a Muslim country that you should accept what Allāh has accepted from them and fulfill the responsibilities which Allāh has accorded them... And there must be a barrier keeping you from doing any injustice to them, from depriving them of the protection of Allāh, and from flaunting the commitments of Allāh and His Messenger concerning them. Because we have been told that the Holy Prophet said, 'Whosoever does injustice to a protected non-Muslim, I will be his enemy (on the Day of Judgement).'"*[6]

Although Islam does not accord to followers of other religions the same recognition that it has accorded to Jews and Christians, it believes in peaceful co-existence with them. One of the earliest messages of peaceful co-existence given by the Prophet Muḥammad to the idol-worshippers of Mecca is reflected in Chapter 109 of the Qur'an: Say: *"O unbelievers! Neither do I worship what you worship; nor do you worship what I worship. Neither am I going to worship what you worship; nor are you going to worship what I worship. To you shall be your religion and to me shall be my religion."*

From the historical perspective, the treatment that Muslim societies have given to the minorities under their rule, especially the Christians and the Jews, is comparatively better than the way minorities were treated in Christian Europe.[7]

While writing about the last Muslim Empire, Ira Lapidus says, "The Ottomans, like previous Muslim regimes, considered the non-Muslim subjects autonomous but dependent peoples whose internal social, religious, and communal life was regulated by their own religious organizations, but their leaders were appointed by, and responsible to, a Muslim state."[8]

Religious Pluralism

The most famous proponent of modern religious pluralism is John Hick, who abandoned his Catholic exclusivist view and formulated his specific theory in the seventies. Hick's pluralistic hypothesis claims that each religion in its own way represents an authentic revelation of the Divine world and a fully authentic means of salvation. He believes that all religions are culturally conditioned responses to the same ultimate reality; and, therefore, are equally valid, and salvation is possible through any of them.

Hick uses the famous story of the Hindu mystics to illustrate his point: "An elephant was brought to a group of blind men who had never encountered such an animal before. One felt a leg and reported that an elephant is a great living pillar. Another felt the trunk and reported that an elephant is a great snake. Another felt a tusk and reported that an elephant is like a sharp ploughshare, and so on. And then they all quarrelled together, each claiming that his own account was the truth and therefore all the others false. In fact of course, they were all true, but each referring only to one aspect of the total reality and all expressed in very imperfect analogies."[9]

There are many flaws in Hick's hypothesis. The most serious problem is of reconciling the conflicting truth-claims of various religions: for example, monotheism of Islam as opposed to polytheism of Hinduism; death and resurrection of Islam and Christianity as opposed to reincarnations and reaching the state of nirvana of Buddhism; salvation through Trinity as opposed to Tawḥīd (Monotheism), etc.

In order to resolve the problem of conflicting truth-claims, Hick suggests that religious traditions differ on three issues: (1) on historical facts; (2) on trans-historical facts; (3) on conceptions of the Real. Then he proposes the solution for these differences.

For the disagreements on **historical facts**, Hick suggests that they are minor issues and they could be resolved by application of the historical method. As for differences on **trans-historical facts** (i.e., matters that cannot be established by historical or empirical evidence such as "is the universe temporal or eternal" or "death and then resurrection versus reincarnations"), he says that the resolution of such differences are not necessary for salvation and that religions need to dialogue more in order to modify their beliefs. For differing **conceptions of the Real**, Hick assumes that all religious traditions are authentic manifestations of the Real and that each tradition's deity is an authentic face of the Real.[10] Finally, Hick believes that any religious belief that would conflict with, and if literally true, falsify another religious belief, must be treated as mythological.

The end result of this theory is that in order to make it workable, Hick would have to redefine many religious beliefs in ways that the founders and followers of those religions would strongly protest! Take the example of the historical status of Jesus from Islamic, Christian and Jewish perspectives:

Concept	**Christianity**	**Islam**	**Judaism**
1. Miraculous birth	Yes	Yes	No
2. Miracles	Yes	Yes	No
3. Status	Messiah & Son of God	Prophet & Messenger	No
4. Revelation	Gospels written by different authors.	Injīl revealed by God to Jesus	No
5. Death and After	Crucified for the redemption of sins and resurrected after three days.	Never crucified; taken to the Heavens.	Crucified and died.

Apart from the two first items (and that also only between Islam and Christianity), all three Abrahamic religions have conflicting views on Jesus. According to John Hick's theory, the first two common beliefs would be considered as "facts" (at the least in Christianity and Islam) whereas the other points of disagreements must be treated in two possible ways: Either these conflicting views should be resolved by historical/empirical inquiry or they should be put in the category of "mythology"! The first solution will force the Jews, the Christians and the Muslims to reject many verses of their respective scriptures while the second solution will place many statements from the Bibl]e and the Qur'an into the category of "mythology". None would be acceptable to any of the three faiths.

I think this one example (that also of Islam vis-à-vis Christianity and Judaism which are closer to one another than Islam vis-à-vis Hinduism and Buddhism) suffices to show that Hick's theory of religious pluralism is not workable.

Based on Hick's solution for meta-historical facts (issues related to death and after), Muslims will be forced to consider more than five hundred verses of the Qur'an on death, resurrection and afterlife as part of "mythology"!

Coming to the third type of differences on conceptions of the Real, Dr. John Hick wants us to believe that the Trinity of Christians, the multiples idols of Hindus, and the *Tawhīd* (Monotheism) of Muslims are equally valid and true! This hypothesis weakens the faith in one's religion and pushes one towards agnosticism if not atheism.

Using Immanuel Kant's view of dualistic categories, Hick says that there is a difference "between an entity as 'it is in itself' and as 'it appears in perception'."[11] Something could be completely true "in itself" but when it is perceived by others, it is relatively true. Based on this idea, Hick wants all religions to accept all differing conceptions of God as equally authentic because none of them are absolutely true, all are only relatively true. The way Hick has used the story of the blind men and the elephant, he has assumed all religious people to be blind and that they lack the ability to know the complete truth. Unfortunately, he has missed the moral of the same story as given by Mawlānā Rūmī:

Some Hindus have an elephant to show.
No one here has ever seen an elephant.
They bring it at night to a dark room.
    One by one, we go in the dark and come out
    saying how we experience the animal.

One of us happens to touch the trunk.
"A water-pipe kind of creature."
    Another, the ear. "A very strong, always moving
    back and forth, fan-animal."
Another, the leg. "I find it still,
like a column on a temple."

    Another touches the curved back.
    "A leathery throne."
Another, the cleverest, feels the tusk.
"A rounded sword made of porcelain."
He's proud of his description.
    Each of us touches one place
    and understands the whole in that way.

The palm and the fingers feeling in the dark are
how the senses explore the reality of the elephant.

If each of us held a candle there,
and if we went in together,
we could see it.[12]

In Hick's story, these men were groping in darkness and, therefore, they came with wrong description of the elephant; if they had used a "candle", they would have seen the light! In Islam, God does not let a searcher for truth grope in darkness: "God is the

Protector of the believers, He brings them forth from the shadows into the light." [13]

The Qur'an and Religious Pluralism

Some Muslim intellectuals have attempted to read the theory of religious pluralism into the Qur'an itself. The most famous argument used by them is that the term "Islam," in the Qur'an, should not be taken as a noun but just as a verb. Sometimes they differentiate between "islam" (the act of submission) and "Islam" (the religion); and say that the main message of God and the basis of salvation is submission to God, and that it does not matter whether the submission takes place through Abraham, Moses, Jesus, or Muḥammad (peace be upon all of them)

This is nothing new; even Āyatullāh Muṭahharī, in the present work, writes, "If someone were to say that the meaning of 'Islam' in this verse is not our religion in particular; rather, the intent is the literal meaning of the word, or submission to God, the answer would be that undoubtedly 'Islam' means submission and the religion of Islam is the religion of submission, but **the reality of submission has a particular form in each age**. And in this age, its form is the same cherished religion that was brought by the Seal of the Prophets (Muḥammad). So it follows that the word 'Islam' (submission) necessarily applies to it alone.

"In other words, the necessary consequence of submission to God is to accept His commandments, and it is clear that one must always act on the *final* Divine commandments. And the final commandments of God is what His final Messenger [Muḥammad] has brought."[14]

"Islam" in the Qur'an [3:19-20]

When the Qur'an says, for example: "Surely the religion with Allāh is al-Islam,"[15], some Muslim intellectuals say that it does not mean "**Islam**" the religion that started in the seventh century by Prophet Muḥammad. They say it means "islām," submission to God through any of the Abrahamic religions.

In their attempt to read a politically correct idea into the Qur'an, they even ignore the context of the verse. Let us read the whole passage together: *"Surely* ***the religion*** *with Allāh is* ***al-Islam.*** *And those who have been given the Book [i.e., the Christians and the Jews] did not show opposition but after knowledge had come to them, out of envy among themselves. And whoever disbelieves in the verses of Allāh, then surely Allāh is quick in reckoning. But if they dispute with you, say:* ***"I have submitted*** *myself entirely to Allāh and (so has)* ***everyone who follows me.*** *And to those who have been given the Book [i.e., the Christians and the Jews] and to the idol-worshippers [of Mecca], say:* ***"Do you submit?"*** *If they* ***submit,*** *then they are* ***rightly guided;*** *but if they reject, then upon you is only the delivery of the message. And Allāh sees the servants."*[16]

This passage clearly states the following:

- "Al-Islam" mentioned in this verse is the message of submission as brought by Prophet Muḥammad.
- The People of the Scripture (i.e., Christians and Jews) are in opposition of this version of submission to God.
- The Prophet Muḥammad and his followers are followers of the Islam which was brought by him.
- The People of the Scripture are being asked to submit to God through Prophet Muḥammad even though they already are followers of Prophets Moses and Jesus.
- The same message is given to the idol-worshippers of Mecca.
- If the People of the Scripture do not submit (as Prophet Muḥammad and his followers have submitted), then they are not "rightly guided".

So the term al-Islam, in this verse, refers to "submission to God" through His final message brought by Prophet Muḥammad and not through previous prophets.

"Islam" in the Qur'an [3:83-85]

Another passage from the same chapter is also relevant for understanding the meaning of "Islam": *"Is it then other than* ***Allāh's religion*** *that they seek while to Him submits whoever is in the heavens and the Earth, willingly or unwillingly, and to Him shall they be returned? Say: "We* ***believe in*** *Allāh, and* ***what has been revealed to us,*** *and what was revealed to Abraham, Ishmael, Isaac,*

Jacob, and the Tribes; and what was given to Moses and Jesus and to the prophets from their Lord. We do not make any distinction between (the claim of) any of them, and ***to Him do we submit****. And whoever desires* ***a religion other than Islam****, it shall not be accepted from him, and in the hereafter he shall be one of the losers."*

This passage clearly explains basic beliefs of Allāh's religion:

- Among those basic beliefs is the requirement to believe in "what has been revealed to us" (i.e., the Qur'an that has been revealed to Muslims).
- "Islam – submission" only follows when one accepts all the prophets and does not differentiate in the truth of any one of them, including Prophet Muḥammad.

"Islam" and "Imān "in the Qur'an [2:135-137]

The following passage in Chapter Two of the Qur'an further clarifies the meaning of "islām–submission" as well as "imān–belief": *"And they say: "Be Jew or Christian and you will be guided aright. Say: "Nay! (we follow) the religion of Abraham, the sincere, and he was not one of the polytheists. Say: "****We believe*** *in Allāh; and* ***in what has been revealed to us****; and in what has been revealed to Abraham, Ishmael, Isaac, Jacob, and the Tribes; and in what was given to Moses and Jesus; and in what has been given to the prophets from their Lord -- we do not differentiate between (the claim) of any of them;* ***and to Him do we submit. If they (i.e., the Jews and the Christians) then believe as you believe, then they are rightly guided;*** *but if they refuse, then they are only in great opposition; and Allāh will suffice you against them. He is the Hearing, the Knowing."*

These two verses clearly define the "imān - faith and belief" of the Muslims as opposed to that of the Jews and the Christians. Central to the imān of the Muslims is belief in the revelation of all the prophets, including the revelation to the Prophet Muhammad.

They clearly say that if the Jews and the Christians "believe as you believe," only then will they be rightly guided.

The second chapter of the Qur'an al-Baqarah (2), Verse 285 also confirms this meaning of "imān": *"The Messenger (i.e., Muḥammad) has believed in whatever that has been revealed to him from his*

Lord; and the believers all believe in Allāh, His Angels, His books, and His messengers. (And they say:) "We do not differentiate between (the claim of) any one of His messengers."

A note on "we do not differentiate between any one of the messengers" or "we do not make any distinction between any one of them": it does not mean that all the prophets and messengers of Allāh are of the same rank and status. We have already mentioned that there are five prophets who rank highest in the spiritual hierarchy. Rather, this means that we do not make any distinction in the truth of any of the prophets; all are equally true in their claim. This is unlike the Jews who accept all the prophets but reject Jesus and Muḥammad or the Christians who accept all the prophets but reject Muḥammad.

"Imān" in the Qur'an [2:62]

The verse which is presented as the most convincing support for religious pluralism is verse 62 of chapter two of the Qur'an: *"Verily the believers, the Jews, the Christians and the Sābaeanes —* ***whoever believes in Allāh and the Last Day, and does good deeds—*** *they shall have their reward with their Lord and neither shall they have fear nor shall they grieve."*

At the initial reading, it might seem that the Muslims (i.e., believers), the Jews, the Christians, and the Sābeans all will gain salvation in the hereafter as long as they believe in God and the Last Day, and do good deeds.

Does this verse say that even the Jews of post-Jesus era and the Christians of post-Muḥammadan era will also gain salvation in the hereafter? This will be a correct understanding only if this verse is studied in isolation without taking the other relevant verses into consideration. Such a loop-sided understanding is not the correct way of studying the Qur'an, as it has been said that some verses of the Qur'an explain some other verses. The loop-sided understanding goes against the clear meanings of the followings verses: *"They are certainly disbelievers who say: 'Messiah, son of Mary, is the God.'"* (5:17) or *"Indeed those who disbelieve from among the People of the Book and the polytheists will be in the fire of hell, to abide therein (forever). It is they who are the worst of creatures."* (98:6) Compare that with the next verse: *"Indeed those who believe and do good deeds – it is they who are the best of creatures: their reward, near their Lord, is the Gardens of Eden with rivers flowing in them, to abide therein (forever). Allāh is pleased with them and they are pleased with Him. That is for those who fear their Lord."*(98:7-8)

In addition: *"Had the People of the Book believed and feared (God), We would surely have absolved them of their misdeeds. Had they observed the Torah (revealed to Moses) and the Evangel (revealed to Jesus), they would surely have drawn nourishment from above them and from beneath their feet."*(5:65-66)

These three verses clearly describe the People of the Scripture as "disbelievers" and go completely opposite the initial meaning of verse 2:62 and as we know, there can be no contradiction in the Qur'an.

So how do we then interpret the verse 2:62?

First of all, verse 2:62 is actually emphasizing the issue of having true belief as opposed to just carrying the label of "Muslim" or "Christian" or "Jew" or "Sābaean". As the sentence in the middle of that verse clarifies, these labels have no value without the sound faith and good deeds.

Secondly, the meaning of "belief, faith-*imān*" in this verse, as supported by verses discussed earlier, includes the belief in the current (or final) Messenger of God. The implication of verse 2:62, in light of the other verses, will have to be curtailed to include only those People of the Scripture who followed the prophet of their own era.

So a Jew who lived during the era of Moses (i.e., before Jesus' advent), is guaranteed salvation provided he believed in Moses' message and followed him faithfully. Similarly, a Christian who lived during the era of Jesus (i.e., before Muḥammad's advent) is guaranteed salvation provided he believed in Jesus' message and followed him faithfully. In other words, a Jew of Moses' era and a Christian of Jesus' era was as much a "believer – *mu'min*" as the Muslim of the Muḥammadan era, and just like him, they also will gain salvation and blessings of God in the hereafter.

However, if a person who lives in the Islamic era and has received the final message of God through Prophet Muḥammad but still does not accept it, then he is definitely not included in the salvation and blessings of verse 2:62. Read the following verse (4:115) which is very decisive in this matter: "But whosoever defies the Messenger (i.e., Muḥammad), after the guidance has become manifest to him, and follows a way other than that of the believers, We shall abandon him to his devices and We shall make him enter hell, and that is an evil destination."

Prophet Muḥammad and Religious Pluralism

Those Muslim intellectuals who preach about religious pluralism in Islam seem to be oblivious of some historical facts of Islamic history and the Prophet's life. If Judaism and Christianity are concurrently valid paths of submission to God, then why did the Prophet Muḥammad work so hard to convey his message even to the Jews and the Christians? If they were already on the Right Path (Ṣirat Mustaqīm), then why did the Prophet feel it important to invite them to Islam?

After the peace treaty of Hudaybiyya in 6 AH, the Prophet of Islam sent emissaries to various rulers and tribes around and beyond the Arabian Peninsula with a distinct purpose of inviting them to Islam. According to historians, around 25 letters were sent by the Prophet to various rulers and tribes.[17]

Among those who were sent to the Christian rulers and tribes, we see the following names: Diḥyah al-Kalbī sent to Heraclius, the Emperor of Byzantine; 'Amr bin Umayyah Zamrī to the Negus, the King of Abyssinia; Ḥāṭib bin Abī Baltā'a sent to the Muqawqis, the King of Egypt; and the tribes of Ghassan and Ḥanīfah (in northern Arabia). Three letters are important and relevant to our discussion.

In his letter to Heraclius, the Byzantine Emperor, the Prophet Muḥammad wrote: *"... Peace be upon him who follows the guidance. I invite you to accept Islam. Accept Islam and you will prosper and Allāh will give you double rewards. But if you refuse, then the sin of your people also will fall upon your shoulders. O' People of the Scripture, come to the word common between us and you that we shall not worship anything but Allāh, and that we shall not associate anything with Him, nor shall some of us take others for lords besides Allāh. But if you turn back, then say: Bear witness that we are Muslims."*

In the letter to the Negus, the King of Abyssinia, the Prophet Muḥammad wrote: *"... Peace be upon him who follows the guidance. Praise be to Allāh besides whom there is no other god, the Sovereign, the Holy One, the Preserver of Peace, the Keeper of the Faithful, the Guardian. I bear witness that Jesus, son of Mary, is indeed a spirit of God and His word, which He conveyed unto the chaste Mary. He created Jesus through His word just as He created Ādam with His hands. And now I call you to Allāh who is One and has no partner, and to friendship in His obedience. Follow me and believe in what has been revealed to me, for I am the Messenger of Allāh. I invite you and your people to Allāh, the Mighty, the Glorious. I have conveyed the message, and it is up to you to accept it. Once again, peace be upon him who follows the path of guidance."*

In the letter sent to the Muqawqis, the King of Egypt and a Coptic Christian, the Prophet Muḥammad wrote: *"...Peace be upon him who follows the guidance. I invite you to accept the message of Islam. Accept it and you shall prosper. But if you turn away, then upon you shall also fall the sin of the Copts. O' People of the Scripture, come to a word common between us and you that we shall worship none but Allāh and that we shall ascribe no partner unto Him and that none of us shall regard anyone as lord besides God. And if they turn away, then say: Bear witness that we are Muslims."*[18]

Even the arrival of the delegation from Christian Najran (Yemen) and how the Prophet invited them to Islam and, finally, how he challenged them to the malediction *(mubāhala)* is in the same spirit of inviting the People of the Book to Islam.

All these letters and the meeting with Najrani Christians prove beyond any doubt that if the People of the Book were on ṣirāt mustaqīm - the right path that leads to salvation - then the Prophet would not have invited them to Islam.

Important Caution

At the conclusion of this introduction, I would like to reiterate the caution that believing in Islam as the only valid path of submission to God does not automatically and necessarily lead to the belief that all non-Muslims will go to hell. Neither does this exclusivist view of Islam as the only sirāt mustaqīm prevent us from promoting tolerance and peaceful co-existence among the followers of various religions, especially the Jews and the Christians.

While talking about polytheist parents, Almighty Allāh says: *"And if they insist on you to associate with Me (someone as on object of worship) of what you have no knowledge, then do not obey them, however interact with them in this world kindly ..."*[19]

Thus, a Muslim has to resist the un-Islamic influence of non-Muslims, but still be kind to them. In other words, although your paths in the hereafter will be separate, that does not prevent you from being kind, merciful, and just to non-Muslims in this world.

Sayyid Muḥammad Rizvi
Toronto, Ontario
March 3rd, 2006

BIOGRAPHY OF THE AUTHOR

Ayatullāh Murtadhā Mutahharī, one of the principle architects of the new Islamic consciousness in Iran, was born on February 2nd, 1920, in Farīmān, then a village and now a township about sixty kilometres from Mashhad, the great centre of Shī'a pilgrimage and learning in Eastern Iran.[20] His father was Muḥammad Ḥusain Mutahharī, a renown scholar who studied in Najaf, Iraq and spent several years in Egypt and Saudi Arabia before returning to Farīmān.

At the exceptionally early age of twelve, Mutahharī began his formal religious studies at the teaching institution in Mashhad, which was then in a state of decline, partly because of internal reasons and partly because of the repressive measures directed by Ridhā Khān, the first Pahlavī autocrat, against all Islamic institutions. But in Mashhad, Mutahharī discovered his great love for philosophy, theology, and mysticism, a love that remained with him throughout his life and came to shape his entire outlook on religion: "I can remember that when I began my studies in Mashhad and was still engaged in learning elementary 'Arabic, the philosophers, mystics, and theologians impressed me far more than other scholars and scientists, such as inventors and explorers. Naturally I was not yet acquainted with their ideas, but I regarded them as heroes on the stage of thought."[21]

For various reasons, Mutahharī left Mashhad to join the growing number of students congregating in the teaching institution in Qum. Thanks to the skilful stewardship of the late scholar 'Abdul Karīm Hā'irī, Qum was on its way to becoming the spiritual and intellectual capital of Islamic Iran, and Mutahharī was able to benefit there from the instruction of a wide range of scholars. He studied Jurisprudence and the Principles of Jurisprudence - the core subjects of the traditional curriculum - with Āyatullāh Ḥujjat Kuhkamarī, Āyatullāh Sayyid Muḥammad Dāmād, Āyatullāh Sayyid Muḥammad Ridhā

Gulpāyagānī, and Ḥajj Sayyid Ṣadr al-Dīn as-Ṣadr. But more important than all these was Āyatullāh Burujerdī, the successor of Ḥā'irī as director of the teaching establishment in Qum. Muṭahharī attended his lectures from his arrival in Qum in 1944 until his departure for Tehran in 1952, and he nourished a deep respect for him.

Fervent devotion and close affinity characterized Muṭahharī's relationship with his prime mentor in Qum, Āyatullāh Rūḥullāh Khumaynī. When Muṭahharī arrived in Qum, Āyatullāh Khumaynī was a young lecturer, but he was already marked out from his contemporaries by the profoundness and comprehensiveness of his Islamic vision and his ability to convey it to others. These qualities were manifested in the celebrated lectures on ethics that he began giving in Qum in the early 1930s.

In 1952, Muṭahharī left Qum for Tehran, where he married the daughter of Āyatullāh Rūḥānī and began teaching philosophy at *Madressah* [Religious school] Marwi, one of the principal institutions of religious learning in the capital. This was not the beginning of his teaching career, for already in Qum he had begun to teach certain subjects - logic, philosophy, theology, and jurisprudence - while still a student himself. But Muṭahharī seems to have become progressively impatient with the somewhat restricted atmosphere of Qum, with the factionalism prevailing among some of the students and their teachers, and with their remoteness from the concerns of society. His own future prospects in Qum were also uncertain.

In Tehran, Muṭahharī found a broader and more satisfying field of religious, educational, and ultimately political activity. In 1954, he was invited to teach philosophy at the Faculty of Theology and Islamic Sciences of Tehran University, where he taught for twenty--two years. First the regularization of his appointment and then his promotion to professor was delayed by the jealousy of mediocre colleagues and by political considerations (for Muṭahharī's closeness to Āyatullāh Khumaynī was well known). But the presence of a figure such as Muṭahharī in the secular university was significant and effective. Many men of Madressah background had come to teach in the universities, and they were often of great erudition. However, almost without exception they had discarded an Islamic worldview, together with their turbans and cloaks. Muṭahharī, by contrast, came to the university as an articulate and convinced exponent of Islamic science and wisdom, almost as an envoy of the religious institution to the secularly educated. Numerous people responded to him, as the pedagogical powers he had first displayed in Qum now fully unfolded.

The spoken word plays in general a more effective and immediate role in promoting revolutionary change than the written word, and it would be possible to compose an anthology of key sermons, addresses, and lectures that have carried the Islamic Revolution of Iran forward. However the clarification of the ideological content of the revolution and its demarcation from opposing or competing schools of thought have necessarily depended on the written word, on the composition of works that expound Islamic doctrine in systematic form, with particular attention to contemporary problems and concerns. In this area, Muṭahharī's contribution was unique in its volume and scope.

Muṭahharī wrote assiduously and continuously, from his student days in Qum up to 1979, the year of his martyrdom. Much of his output was marked by the a philosophical tone and emphasis, and he probably regarded as his most important work "The Principles of Philosophy and the Method of Realism", the record of his teacher 'Allāmah Ṭabā'ṭabā'ī's discourses to the Thursday evening circle in Qum, supplemented with Muṭahharī's comments. But he did not choose the topics of his books in accordance with personal interest or predilection, but with his perception of need; wherever a book was lacking on some vital topic of contemporary Islamic interest, Muṭahharī sought to supply it.

Single handily, he set about constructing the main elements of a contemporary Islamic library. Books such as "The Divine Justice", "The System of Women's Rights in Islam", "The Question of the Veil", "An Introduction to the Islamic Sciences", and "An Introduction to the Worldview of Islam" were all intended to fill a need, to contribute to an accurate and systematic understanding of Islam and the problems in the Islamic society.

These books may well come to be regarded as Muṭahharī's most lasting and important contribution to the rebirth of Islamic Iran, but his activity also had a political dimension that admittedly subordinate, should not be overlooked. While a student and fledgling teacher in Qum, he had sought to instill political consciousness in his contemporaries and was particularly close to those among them who were members of the Fida'iyan-i Islam, the Militant Organization founded in 1945 by Nawwab Safawī. The Qum headquarters of the Fida'iyan was the Madrasa-yi Fayziya, where Muṭahharī himself resided, and he sought in vain to prevent them from being removed from the Madressah by Āyatullāh Burūjerdī, who was resolutely set against all political confrontation with the Shah's regime.

His first serious confrontation with the Shah's regime came during the uprising of June 6th, 1963, when he showed himself to be politically, as well as intellectually, a follower of Āyatullāh Khumaynī by distributing his declarations and urging support for him in the sermons he gave.[22] He was accordingly arrested and held for forty-three days. After his release, he participated actively in the various organizations that came into being to maintain the momentum that had been created by the uprising, most importantly the Association of Militant Religious Scholars. In November 1964, Āyatullāh Khumaynī entered on his fourteen years of exile, spent first in Turkey and then in Najaf, Iraq, and throughout this period Muṭahharī remained in touch with Āyatullāh Khumaynī, both directly - by visits to Najaf - and indirectly.

When the Islamic Revolution approached its triumphant climax in the winter of 1978 and Āyatullāh Khumaynī left Najaf for Paris, Muṭahharī was among those who travelled to Paris to meet and consult with him. His closeness to Āyatullāh Khumaynī was confirmed by his appointment to the Council of the Islamic Revolution, the existence of which Āyatullāh Khumaynī announced on January 12th, 1979.

Muṭahharī's services to the Islamic Revolution were brutally curtailed by his assassination on May 1st, 1979. The murder was carried out by a group known as Furqān, which claimed to be the protagonists of a "progressive Islam," one freed from the allegedly distorting influence of the religious scholars. Although Muṭahharī appears to have been chairman of the Council of the Islamic Revolution at the time of his assassination, it was as a thinker and a writer that he was martyred.

On Tuesday, May 1, 1979, Muṭahharī went to the house of Dr. Yadullāh Saḥābī, in the company of other members of the Council of the Islamic Revolution. At about 10:30 at night, he and another participant in the meeting, Engineer Katira'i, left Saḥābī's house. Walking by himself to an adjacent alley where the car that was to take him home was parked, Muṭahharī suddenly heard an unknown voice call out to him. He looked around to see where the voice was coming from, and as he did, a bullet struck him in the head, entering beneath the right earlobe and exiting above the left eyebrow. He died almost instantly, and although he was rushed to a nearby hospital, there was nothing that could be done but mourn for him. The body was left in the hospital the following day, and then on Thursday, amid widespread mourning, it was taken for funeral prayers first to Tehran University and then to Qum for burial, next to the grave of 'Abdul Karīm Hā'irī.

Āyatullāh Khumaynī wept openly when Muṭahharī was buried in Qum, and he described him as his "dear son," and as "the fruit of my life," and as "a part of my flesh." But in his eulogy Āyatullāh Khumaynī also pointed out that with the murder of Muṭahharī neither his personality was diminished, nor was the course of the revolution interrupted: "Let the evil-wishers know that with the departure of Muṭahharī - his Islamic personality, his philosophy and learning, have not left us. Assassinations cannot destroy the Islamic personality of the great men of Islam...Islam grows through sacrifice and martyrdom of its cherished ones. From the time of its revelation up to the present time, Islam has always been accompanied by martyrdom and heroism."[23]

The personage and legacy of Āyatullāh Muṭahharī have certainly remained unforgotten in the Islamic Republic, to such a degree that his posthumous presence has been almost as impressive as the attainments of his life. The anniversary of his martyrdom is regularly commemorated, and his portrait is ubiquitous throughout Iran. Many of his unpublished writings are being printed for the first time, and the whole corpus of his work is now being distributed and studied on a massive scale. In the words of Āyatullāh Khamene'ī, leader of the Islamic Republic, the works of Muṭahharī have come to constitute "the intellectual infrastructure of the Islamic Republic."

Efforts are accordingly under way to promote a knowledge of Muṭahharī's writings outside the Persian-speaking world as well, and the Ministry of Islamic Guidance has sponsored translations of his works into languages as diverse as Spanish and Malay. In a sense, however, it will be the most fitting memorial to Muṭahharī if revolutionary Iran proves able to construct a polity, society, economy and culture that are authentically and integrally Islamic. For Muṭahharī's life was oriented to a goal that transcended individual motivation, and his martyrdom was the final expression of that effacement of self.

GOOD DEEDS OF NON MUSLIMS

Outline of the Discussion

One of the issues which is discussed regarding "Divine justice" is the issue of the good deeds performed by non-Muslims. Today, the issue of whether the good deeds of non-Muslims are accepted by God or not is under discussion amongst the different classes - whether learned or unlearned, literate or illiterate. If they are accepted, what difference does it make if a person is a Muslim or not; the important thing is to do good in this world. If a person is not a Muslim and practices no religion, he or she has lost nothing. And if their actions are not acceptable and are altogether void with no reward or recompense from God, then how is that compatible with Divine justice?

This same question can be asked from a Shī'a perspective within the bounds of Islam: Are the actions of a non-Shī'a Muslim acceptable to God, or are they null and void? If they are acceptable, what difference does it make if a person is a Shī'a Muslim or a non-Shī'a Muslim? What is important is to be Muslim; a person who is not a Shī'a and doesn't believe in the *wilāyah*[24] (Divinely-appointed guardianship) of the *Ahlul Bait* (the specifically designated family members of the Prophet Muhammad) has not lost anything. And if the actions of such a person are not acceptable to God, then how is that compatible with Divine justice?

In the past, this issue was only discussed by philosophers and in the books of philosophy. However, today it has entered into the minds of all levels of society; few people can be found who have not at least broached the subject for themselves and in their own minds.

Divine philosophers would discuss the issue from the aspect that if all people who are outside the fold of religion are to face perdition and Divine punishment, it necessarily follows that in the universe, evil and compulsion are preponderant. However, the fact that felicity and good have primacy in the universe - not evil and wretchedness – is an accepted and definitive principle.

Humanity is the greatest of all of creation; everything else has been created for it (of course, with the correct conception of this idea that is understood by the wise, not the perception that the short-sighted people commonly possess). If humanity itself is to be created for the Hell-fire – that is, if the final abode of the majority of humanity is to be Hell – then one must grant that the anger of God supersedes His mercy. This is because the majority of people are strangers to the true religion; and even those who are within the fold of the true religion are beset by deviation and digression when it comes to practicing. This was the background of the discussion amongst the philosophers.

It has been nearly half a century that, as a result of easier communication among Muslim and non-Muslim nations, an increase in the means of communication, and greater interaction amongst nations, the issue of whether being a Muslim and a believer as a necessary condition for the acceptability of good deeds is being discussed among all levels of society, especially the so-called intellectuals.

When these people study the lives of inventors and scientists of recent times who were not Muslim but who performed valuable services for humanity, they find such people worthy of reward. On the other hand since they used to think that the actions of non-Muslims are altogether null and void, they fall into serious doubt and uncertainty. In this way, an issue which for years was the exclusive domain of the philosophers has entered the general conversations of people and has taken the form of an objection with regard to Divine justice.

Of course, this objection is not directly related to Divine justice; it is related to Islam's viewpoint about human beings and their actions, and becomes related to Divine justice inasmuch as it appears that such a viewpoint regarding human beings, their actions, and God's dealing with them is in opposition to the standards of Divine justice.

In the interactions that I have and have had with students and the youth, I have frequently been faced with this question.

Sometimes they ask whether the great inventors and scientists, with all the worthy services which they have done for humanity, will go to Hell. Will the likes of Pasteur and Edison go to Hell while indolent holy people who have spent their lives idly in a corner of the Mosque go to Heaven? Has God created Heaven solely for us Shīʿas?

I remember that once an acquaintance from my city, who was a practicing Muslim, came to Tehran to visit me, and he raised this issue.

This man had visited a lepers' hospital in Mashhad and had been stirred and deeply affected by the sight of the Christian nurses who were sincerely (at least in his view) looking after the patients with leprosy. At that time, this issue came up in his mind and he fell into doubt.

You are aware that looking after a patient of leprosy is a very difficult and unpleasant task and when this hospital was established in Mashhad, very few doctors were willing to serve there, and similarly, no one was willing to care for the patients. Advertisements for the employment of nurses were taken out in the newspapers; in all of Iran, not a single person gave a positive answer to this invitation. A small group of so-called ascetic Christian women from France came and took charge of nursing the lepers.

This man, who had seen the humanitarianism and loving care of those nurses towards lepers, who had been abandoned by even their own parents, had been strongly affected by these nurses.

He related that the Christian nurses wore long, loose clothes, and apart from their face and hands, no part of their body was visible. Each of them had a long rosary - which had perhaps a thousand beads - and whenever they would find free time from work, they would busy themselves in their recitations on the rosary.

Then the man asked with a troubled mind and in a disturbed tone whether it was true that non-Muslims would not enter Heaven?

Of course, right now we are not concerned with the motives of those Christian ladies. Was it truly for God, in God's way, and out of pure humanitarianism that they did what they did, or was another motive in play? Certainly, we don't want to be pessimistic, just as we are not overly optimistic; our point is that these incidents and events have introduced our people to a serious question.

Several years ago, I was invited to an association to give a speech. In that association, in accordance with their tradition, the participants were requested to write down any questions they had so that they could be answered at the appropriate time. Those questions had been recorded in a notebook, and that notebook had been given to me so I could choose the topic of my speech from amongst those topics (noted in the book). I noticed that the question that had been repeated more than any other was whether God will send all non-Muslims to Hell. Will Pasteur, Edison, and Kokh be amongst those who will be punished in the Hereafter?

It was from that time that I realized the importance of this issue inasmuch as it had attracted people's thoughts.

Now, in this part of the book, we will discuss this issue. But before we begin, we need to clarify two points in order for the topic at hand to become completely clear.

1. The General Aspect of the Discussion

The purpose of this discussion is not to clarify the status of individuals, for example to specify whether Pasteur will go to Heaven or Hell. What do we know about his true thoughts and beliefs? What were his true intentions? What were his personal and moral traits; and in fact what was the sum of all his actions? Our familiarity with him is limited to his intellectual services, and that is all.

This doesn't apply only to Pasteur. As a matter of principle, the status of individuals is in the hands of God; no one has the right to express an opinion with certainty about whether someone will go to Heaven or Hell. If we were to be asked, "Is the scholar (Shaykh) Murtaḍhā al-Anṣārī[25], in view of his known asceticism, piety, faith, and deeds, definitely among the inhabitants of Heaven?" our answer would be, "From what we know of the man, in his intellectual and practical affairs we haven't heard of anything bad. What we know of him is virtue and goodness. But as to say with absolute certainty whether he will go to Heaven or Hell, that isn't our prerogative. It is

God who knows the intentions of all people, and He knows the secrets and hidden things of all souls; and the account of all people's actions is also with Him. We can only speak with certainty about those whose final outcome has been made known by the religious authorities."

Sometimes people discuss and debate amongst themselves about who was the most virtuous and excellent among the Scholars in terms of nearness to God. For example, was it Sayyid ibne Ṭāwūs[26], or Sayyid Baḥrul 'Ulūm[27], or Shaykh al-Anṣārī? Sometimes they ask about the most eminent among the descendents of the appointed leaders after the Prophet Muḥammad. For example, is Sayyid 'Abdul 'Adhīm al-Hasanī[28] superior in God's view, or Sayyidah Fāṭimah al-Ma'ṣūmah[29]?

Once, one of the Jurisprudents was asked whether 'Abbās b. 'Alī[30] was superior or 'Alī al-Akbar[31]. In order to give the question the form of a practical issue so the Jurisprudent would be compelled to answer it, they asked, "If someone vows to sacrifice a sheep for the most superior of the Imāms' descendents, what is his duty? Is 'Abbās b. 'Alī superior, or 'Alī al-Akbar?"

It is obvious that such discussions are improper, and answering such questions is neither the duty of a *Faqīh* (scholar of Islamic law), nor of anyone else. Specifying the rank of God's creation is not our responsibility. It should be left to God, and no one has any knowledge about the matter except through God himself.

In the early era of Islam, there were instances when people expressed such unjustified opinions, and the Prophet Muḥammad forbade them from doing so.

When 'Uthmān b. Ma'zūn[32] died, a woman of the *Anṣār* (those who had accepted the message of Prophet Muḥammad and requested him to migrate to the city of Madīnah) named Umme 'Alī, who apparently was the wife of the man in whose house 'Uthmān b. Ma'zūn was staying and whose guest he was, addressed his bier in the presence of the Prophet Muḥammad and said: "May heaven be pleasant for you!"

Although 'Uthmān b. Ma'zūn was an eminent man, and the Prophet Muḥammad cried heavily at his funeral and threw himself over the bier and kissed him, the inappropriate statement of that woman displeased him. He turned to her and with an unhappy look said, "How did you know? Why did you make a statement out of ignorance? Have you received a revelation, or do you know the accounts of God's creation?" The woman replied, "O Messenger of God, he was your companion and a brave warrior!" The Noble Messenger answered her with interesting words that are worthy of attention, he said: "I am the Messenger of God, yet I don't know what will be done with me."[33]

This sentence is the exact purport of a verse of the Qur'an: "Say, 'I am not a novelty among the apostles, nor do I know what will be done with me, or with you."[34 35]

A similar incident has also been related regarding the death of Sa'd b. Mu'ādh. In that instance, when the mother of Sa'd said a similar sentence over his coffin, the Messenger said to her, "Be silent; don't make a decision with certainty in God's affairs."[36]

2. No Religion Except al-Islam is Accepted

The other point that must be made clear before beginning the discussion is that the topic of the non-Muslims' good deeds can be discussed in two ways and in reality, is two discussions: First, is any religion other than Islam acceptable to God, or is Islam the only acceptable religion? That is, is it necessary only for a person to have some religion or at most follow a religion associated with one of the Divine prophets, without it then making a difference which religion that is, for example, whether one be a Muslim, Christian, Jew, or even a Zoroastrian? Or is there only one true religion in each era?

After we have accepted that the true religion in each era is only one, the other discussion is whether a person who doesn't follow the true religion but performs a good deed, one that is actually good and is also sanctioned by the true religion, is worthy of reward or not? In other words, is faith in the true religion a condition for one's good deeds to merit reward?

What will be discussed here is the second issue.

With respect to the first issue, we can say briefly that there is only one true religion in each era, and all are obligated to believe in it.

The idea that has recently become common among some so-called intellectuals to the effect that all Divine religions have equal validity in all eras is a fallacious one.

Of course, it is true that there is no disagreement or contradiction among the prophets of God. All of the prophets of God call towards a single goal and the same God. They have not come to create mutually contradicting groups and sects among humanity.

But this doesn't mean that in every era there are several true religions, and thus people in each era can then choose whichever religion they want. To the contrary, it means that a person must believe in all of the Prophets and affirm that each Prophet would give tidings of the Prophet to come, especially the final and greatest of them; and likewise, each Prophet would affirm the previous one. Thus, the necessary consequence of believing in all of the Prophets is to submit in every era to the religion of the Prophet of the time. And of course, it is necessary that in the final era we act on the final commands that have been revealed by God to the final Prophet. And this is what necessarily follows from Islam, that is, submission to God and acceptance of the missions of His Messengers.

Many people in our day have subscribed to the view that it is sufficient for a person to worship God and be affiliated with and practice one of the Divine religions that was revealed by God; the form of the commandments is not that important. Jesus was a Prophet, Muḥammad was also a Prophet; if we follow the religion of Jesus and go to church once a week, that is fine, and if we follow the religion of the final Messenger and pray five times a day, that is also correct. These people say that what is important is for a person to believe in God and practice one of the Divine religions.

George Jordac, author of the book, Imām ʿAlī; Gibrān Khalīl Gibrān, the well-known Lebanese Christian author; and others like them have such a view.[37] These two individuals speak of the Prophet Muḥammad and ʿAlī – and especially the Commander of the Faithful [ʿAlī] – just as a Muslim would.

Some people ask how these people, in spite of their belief in ʿAlī and the Prophet Muḥammad, are still Christian. If they were truthful, they would have become Muslims, and since they haven't done so, it is clear there is something behind the curtain. They are being deceptive, and they aren't sincere in their expression of love and belief in the Prophet Muḥammad and ʿAlī.

The answer is that they are not without sincerity in their expression of love and belief in the Prophet Muḥammad and ʿAlī. However, they have their own way of thinking regarding practicing a religion.

These individuals believe that human beings are not held to a particular religion; any religion is sufficient. Thus, at the same time that they are Christians, they consider themselves admirers and friends of ʿAlī, and they even believe that he himself held their view. George Jordac says, "ʻAlī declines to compel people to necessarily follow a particular religion."

However, we consider this idea void. It is true that "There is no compulsion in religion"[38] however this doesn't mean that there is more than one religion in every age that is acceptable to God, and we have the right to choose any one we please. This is not the case; in every age, there is one true religion and no more. Whenever a Prophet was sent by God with a new religion, the people were obligated to avail themselves of his teachings and learn his laws and commandments, whether in acts of worship or otherwise, until the turn of the Seal of the Prophets came. In this (current) age, if someone wishes to come near God, he or she must seek guidance from the precepts of the religion he brought.

The Noble Qurʾan says: "And whoever desires a religion other than Islam, it shall never be accepted from him, and in the hereafter he shall be among the losers."[39]

If someone were to say that the meaning of "Islam" in this verse is not our religion in particular; rather, the intent is the literal meaning of the word, or submission to God, the answer would be that without doubt Islam means submission and the religion of Islam is the religion of submission, but the reality of submission has a particular form in each age. And in this age, its form is the same cherished religion that was brought by the Seal of the Prophets. So it follows that the word Islam (submission) necessarily applies to it alone.

In other words, the necessary consequence of submission to God is to accept His commandments, and it is clear that one must always act on the final Divine commandments. And the final commandment of God is what His final messenger has brought.

Good Deeds Without Faith

It has become clear that, first of all, our discussion has a general aspect, and we don't want to pass decisions about individuals.

Second, our discussion is not about whether the true religion is one or several; rather, we have accepted that the true religion is one and that all are obligated to accept it.

Third, our discussion is this: if a person, without accepting the true religion, performs a deed which the true religion considers good, does that person receive a reward for that good deed or not?

For example, the true religion has emphasized doing good to others. This includes cultural services like establishing schools, places of learning, writing, and teaching; health services like medicine, nursing, establishing sanitary establishments, and so forth; social services such as mediating disputes, helping the poor and disabled, supporting the rights of the exploited, fighting the exploiters and oppressors, assisting the deprived, establishing justice which is the aim and goal of the Prophets' mission, providing the means of satisfaction for the broken-hearted and misfortunate, and such like. Every religion and every Prophet has enjoined these things. In addition, the reasoning and conscience of each individual rules that these things are good and worthy.

Now, we ask whether a non-Muslim is rewarded if he or she performs such services. The true religion says to be trustworthy and not lie; if a non-Muslim acts in accordance with this principle, will he or she be rewarded or not? In other words, is it equal with respect to a non-Muslim to be trustworthy or treacherous? Are adultery and prayers equal with respect to him or her? This is the issue that we wish to discuss.

Two Ways of Thinking

Normally, those with an intellectual inclination say with certainty that there is no difference between a Muslim and non-Muslim, and even between a monotheist and non-monotheist; whoever performs a good deed, a service like establishing a charitable organization or an invention or something else, deserves recompense from God.

They say that God is Just, and a God who is Just does not discriminate among His servants. What difference does it make for God whether His servant recognizes Him or not or believes in Him or not? Certainly, God will not ignore the good deeds or waste the reward of a person simply because that person doesn't have a relationship of familiarity and love with Him. And even more certainly, if a person believes in God and does good deeds, but does not recognize His Messengers and thus does not have a relationship of familiarity and covenant of friendship with them, God will not cancel out and nullify his or her good deeds.

Directly opposite to these people are those who consider almost all people worthy of punishment and believe in a good end and accepted actions with respect to only a few. They have a very simple standard; they say that people are either Muslim or non-Muslim. Non-Muslims, who are about three-fourths of the world's population, shall go to Hell because they are non-Muslims. The Muslims in their turn are either Shīʿa or non-Shīʿa. The non-Shīʿas, who are about three-fourths of all Muslims, will go to Hell because they are non-Shīʿas. And of the Shīʿas, too, a majority - about three-fourths - are only Shīʿa in name, and it is a small minority that is familiar with even the first obligation, which is to perform *taqlīd* (follow the religious rulings of a particular scholar) of a Jurisprudent, let alone their remaining obligations, and the correctness and completeness of those obligations depends on this obligation. And even those who perform *taqlīd* are for the most part non-practicing. Thus, there are very few who will achieve salvation.

This is the logic of the two sides: the logic of those who, it can almost be said, are absolute conciliation, and the logic of those who we can say are a manifestation of Divine anger, giving anger precedence over mercy.

The Third Logic

Here there is a third logic, which is the logic of the Qur'an. In this issue, the Qur'an gives us a concept that is different from the previous two ideas and that is peculiar to it. The Qur'an's view accords with neither the nonsensical idea of our so-called intellectuals, nor with the narrow-mindedness of our holier-than-thou pious people. The Qur'an's view is rooted in a special logic that everyone, after learning of it, will admit is the correct position in this matter. And this fact increases our faith in this astonishing and remarkable Book and shows that its lofty teachings are independent of the worldly thoughts of human beings and have a celestial source.

Here we present the proofs of both disputing groups (the so-called intellectuals and the so-called pious) and investigate them so that by critiquing them we can slowly arrive at the third logic in regard to this issue, that is, the logic and particular philosophy of the Qur'an.

The So-Called Intellectuals

This group brings two types of proofs for their view: rational and narrational.

1. Rational proof. The rational demonstration that says that good deeds entail their reward no matter who performs them is based on two premises:

The first premise: God has an equal relation to all existent beings. His relation to all times and places is the same; just as God is in the East, He is in the West, and just as He is above, He is below. God is in the present, past and future; the past, present, and future have no difference for God, just as above and below and East and West are the same for Him. Similarly His servants and creation are also the same for Him; He has neither family ties nor a special relationship with anyone. Thus, God's showing grace or showing anger towards people is also the same, except when there are differences in the people themselves.[40]

As a result, no one is dear to God without reason, and no one is lowly or outcast without justification. God has neither ties of kinship nor of nationality with anyone; and no one is the beloved or chosen one of God.

Since God's relation to all beings is the same, there remains no reason for a good deed to be accepted from one person and not from another. If the actions are the same, their reward will also be the same, since the assumption is that God's relation to all people is the same. So justice demands that God reward all those who do good – whether Muslims or non-Muslims – in the same way.

The second premise: The goodness or badness of actions is not based on convention, but on actual reality. In the terminology of scholars of theology and the science of principles of jurisprudence, the "goodness" or "badness" of actions is innate. That is, good and bad deeds are differentiated by their essence; good deeds are good by their essence, and bad deeds are bad by their essence. Honesty, virtue, doing good, helping others, and so forth are good by their essence; and lying, stealing, and oppression are bad by their essence. The goodness of "honesty" or badness of "lying" is not because God has mandated the former and forbidden the latter. To the contrary, it is because "honesty" is good that God has obligated it and because "lying" is bad that God has forbidden it. In short, God's commanding or forbidding is based on the goodness or badness of actions in their essence, and not the other way around.

From these two premises, we conclude that since God does not discriminate, and since good deeds are good from all people, whoever does a good deed will definitely and necessarily be rewarded by God.

It is exactly the same way with regard to evil deeds since there is no difference between those who commit them.

2. Narrational proof. The Qur'an affirms in many verses the principle of non-discrimination among people in rewarding good deeds and punishing evil deeds – which was mentioned in the above rational proof.

The Qur'an strongly opposed the Jews, who believed in such discrimination. The Jews believed – and still believe – that the Jewish race is chosen by God; they would say, "We are the sons and friends of God. Supposing God sends us to Hell, it will not be for more than a limited time."

The Qur'an calls such ideas wishes and untrue thoughts and has strongly combated them. The Qur'an also points out the error of Muslims who have fallen prey to such deception. Here are some of the verses in this regard: "And they said, the Fire shall not touch us except for (a few) numbered days. Say: have you taken a covenant with God, for God shall not violate His covenant, or do you attribute to God that which you don't know? Nay, those who earn evil and whose mistakes have enveloped them are the inhabitants of the Fire; they shall abide therein forever. And those who believe and do good are the inhabitants of Paradise; they shall abide therein forever."[41]

2. In another place, the Qur'an says in answer to the conjecture of the Jews: "And their forgeries deceived them in their religion. So how will they be when We gather them for a day in which there is no doubt and every soul shall be given in full what it has earned; and they shall not be wronged."[42]

3. In another place, the Christians have been added to the Jews, and together they have been opposed by the Qur'an: "And they said, None shall enter Paradise except those who are Jews or Christians; this is their fancy. Say: bring your proof, if you are truthful. Rather, those who submit themselves to God and do good shall have their reward with their Lord; and they shall have no fear, nor shall they grieve."[43]

4. In the forth chapter of the Qur'an, the Muslims too, have been added to the Jews and Christians. The Qur'an demolishes discriminatory thinking no matter who it is from. It is as though the Muslims had come under the effect of the thinking of the People of the Book, and in the face of they who without reason considered themselves superior, adopted such an opinion about themselves. The Qur'an says, refuting these immature fancies: "(This) shall not be in accordance with your vain desires nor in accordance with the vain desires of the followers of the Book. Whoever does evil, he shall be requited with it. He will find for himself neither a guardian nor a helper other than God. And whoever does good deeds whether male

or female and he (or she) is a believer, it is these who shall enter paradise and they will not be wronged (so much as) the speck on a date stone."[44]

5. Leaving aside the verses that condemn baseless suppositions of honour and nearness to God, there are other verses that say that God does not waste the reward of any good deed.

These verses have also been taken as proof of the acceptance of the good deeds of all people, whether Muslim or non-Muslim. In the ninety-ninth chapter of the Qur'an, we read: "So whoever does an atom's weight of good shall see it, and whoever does an atom's weight of evil shall see it."[45]

Elsewhere, God says: "Verily God does not waste the reward of those who do good."[46]

And in another place, He says: "Verily We do not waste the reward of those who do good."[47]

The wording of these verses makes them universal statements that are not given to exceptions.

The scholars of the discipline of the Principles of Jurisprudence say that certain universal statements do not accept exceptions; that is, the wording and tone of the universal statement is such that it resists any exceptions. When it is said, "We don't waste the reward of the doer of good," it means that God's divinity demands that He preserve good deeds; thus it is impossible for God to disregard His divinity in one instance and waste a good deed.

6. There is another verse which is frequently referred to in this discussion, and it is said that it clearly points to the assertion of this group: "Indeed the faithful, the Jews, the Sabaeans, and the Christians—those who have faith in God and the Last Day and act righteously—they will have no fear, nor will they grieve."[48]

In this verse, three conditions have been mentioned for salvation and safety from God's punishment: belief in God, belief in the Day of Judgement, and good deeds; no other condition is mentioned.

Some who are apparently intellectuals have gone one step further and said that the aim of the Prophets was to call towards justice and goodness, and in accordance with the rule "Comply with the spirit and not the letter of the law" we should say that justice and goodness are accepted even from those who don't believe in God and the Day of Judgement. Thus, those who don't believe in God and the Day of Judgement but have made great cultural, medical, economical, or political contributions to humanity shall have a great reward.

Of course, these people can argue on the basis of verses like: "We don't waste the reward of one who does good," and: "So whoever does an atom's weight of good shall see it," but verses like the one above contradict their assertion.

Below we take a look at the proofs of the other group.

The Rigid Group

In opposition to the supposed intellectuals who claim that good deeds are accepted by God from all people in all situations are the "rigid pious ones"; their position is directly opposite to the former group. They say that it is impossible for a non-Muslim's actions to be accepted. The actions of unbelievers and similarly those of non-Shīʿa Muslims have absolutely no value. The non-Muslim and non-Shīʿa Muslim himself is rejected and rebuffed; his actions are even more worthy of being rejected. This group also brings two proofs: rational and narrated.

Rational proof: The rational proof of this group is that if it is supposed that the actions of non-Muslims and non-Shīʿa Muslims are to be accepted by God, what is the difference between Muslims and non-Muslims? The difference between them should be either for the good deeds of Muslims and Shīʿas to be accepted to the exclusion of non-Muslims and non-Shīʿa Muslims, or for the evil deeds of Muslims and Shīʿas not to be punished, again to the exclusion of non-Muslims and non-Shīʿa Muslims. But if we suppose that the good deeds of both groups entail reward and the evil deeds of both groups lead to punishment, what difference will there be between them? And what is the effect of being Muslim or Shīʿa in such a case? The equality of Muslims and non-Muslims, and similarly Shīʿas and non-Shīʿas, in accounting for their actions means that in essence practicing Islam or Shīʿaism is unnecessary and without effect.

Narrated proof: In addition to the above reasoning, this group also argues from two Qur'anic verses and several traditions.

In a few verses of the Qur'an, it has been clearly stated that the actions of unbelievers are not accepted; similarly, in many traditions it has been said that the actions of non-Shīʿas – that is, those who do not have the *wilāyah* (Divinely-ordained guardianship) of the Ahlul Bait – are not accepted.

In the fourteenth chapter of the Qur'an, God compares the actions of unbelievers to ashes which are scattered by a strong wind and lost: "A parable of those who defy their Lord: their deeds are like ashes over which the wind blows hard on a tempestuous day: they have no power over anything they have earned. That is extreme error."[49]

In a verse contained in the twenty-fourth chapter of the Qur'an, the actions of unbelievers have been likened to a mirage which appears to be water but upon being approached, turns out to be nothing.

This verse says that great deeds that give people pause and, in the view of some simpleminded people, are greater than the services of even the Prophets are all null and void if they are not coupled with belief in God. Their greatness is nothing but a fancy, like a mirage. The words of the verse are as below: "As for the faithless, their works are like a mirage in a plain, which the thirsty man supposes to be water. When he comes to it, he finds it to be nothing; but there he finds God, who will pay him his full account, and God is swift at reckoning."[50]

This is the parable of the good deeds of unbelievers, which appear outwardly to be good. So woe upon their evil deeds! We read their parable in the following verse in these words: "Or like the manifold darkness in a deep sea, covered by billow upon billow, overcast by clouds, manifold [layers of] darkness, one on the top of another: when he brings out his hand, he can hardly see it, and one whom God has not granted any light has no light."[51]

By adding this verse to the previous verse, we deduce that the good deeds of unbelievers, with all their deceptive appearances, are a mirage that lacks reality. And as for their evil deeds, alas! They are evil above evil, darkness upon darkness!

The above verses clarify the status of the deeds of unbelievers.

As for non-Shī'a Muslims, from the point of view of us Shī'as, the traditions that have reached us from the Ahlul Bait clarify their position.

Many traditions have reached us on this topic. Those interested can refer to the collection of traditions entitled *al-Kāfī*[52], Volume 1, "The Book of the Divine Proof - *Kitāb al-Ḥujjah*," and Volume 2, "The Book of Belief and Disbelief - *Kitāb al-Īmān wa 'l-Kufr*"; the work, *Wasā'ilush Shī'a*[53], Volume 1, "The Sections on the Introduction to Worship - *Abwāb Muqaddamāt al-'Ibādāt*"; the work, *Mustadrakul Wasā'il*[54], Volume 1, "The Sections on the Introduction to Worship - *Abwāb Muqaddamāt al-'Ibādāt*"; and the work *Biḥārul Anwār*[55], "Discussions about Resurrection," Chapter 17 (Chapter on the Promise, Threat, Invalidation of Actions, and Atonement), and Volume 7 of the old print, Chapter 227, and Volume 15 of the old print, section on ethics, Page 187. As an example, we relate one tradition from *Wasā'ilush Shī'a*:

Muḥammad b. Muslim said, "I heard Imām Muḥammad al-Bāqir[56] say, "Whoever worships God and tires himself in worship but doesn't recognize the Imām (leader) God has appointed for him, his deeds are not accepted, and he himself is astray and lost, and God abhors his actions... and if he dies in this state, he dies not in the state of Islam, but in a state of unbelief and hypocrisy. O Muḥammad b. Muslim, know that the leaders of oppression and their followers are outside the religion of God. They themselves went astray, and they led others astray. Their actions are like ashes which are caught in a strong wind on a stormy day, and they cannot reach anything out of what they have earned. That is the distant deviation."[57]

These are the proofs of those who say that the basis of salvation is faith and belief.

Occasionally, some from this group go to extremes and consider simply the claim of having faith, or in reality a simple affiliation, to be the criterion of Judgement. For example, the Murjī'ī sect in the era of Umayyad Dynasty propagated this idea, and fortunately, with the decline of Umayyad Dynasty, they also ceased to exist. In that age, the Shī'a position, inspired by the Imāms from the Ahlul Bait, was opposite to the Murjī' one, but unfortunately the Murjī'īs' view has lately taken hold in new clothing among some of the common Shī'as.

Some simpleminded Shī'as consider mere apparent affiliation with 'Alī to be sufficient for salvation, and this idea is the basic factor behind the Shī'as' poor state in the modern era. The dervishes and Sufis of the recent era malign good deeds in a different way and under a different pretext; they have made the issue of goodness of heart a pretext, even though true goodness of heart encourages and affirms deeds rather than conflicting with them.

As opposed to these groups, there are others who have raised the value of deeds to such a point that they say that one who commits a major sin is an unbeliever. Such a belief was held by the Khārijites. Some theologians considered the committer of major sins to be neither a believer nor unbeliever, and held that there is a "state between the two states (of belief and unbelief)."

Our task is to see which of these positions is correct. Should we believe in the primacy of belief or the primacy of action? Or is there a third path?

To begin, let us discuss the value of belief and faith.

Value of Belief

With regard to the value of belief, the discussion should proceed in three stages:

1. Is lack of belief in the principles of religion, such as the Oneness of God, Prophecy, and resurrection – and according to the Shī'a view, these three in addition to Divine justice and Imāmate (succession) – always and necessarily cause for Divine punishment? Or is it possible for some unbelievers to be excused and not be punished for their unbelief?

2. Is belief a necessary condition for the acceptance of good deeds, such that no good deed of a non-Muslim or non-Shī'a is acceptable to God?

3. Do unbelief and rejection of the truth cause the invalidity of good deeds or not?

In the coming discussions, we will touch on each of these three stages.

Being Held Accountable For Unbelief

There is no doubt that unbelief is of two types: One is unbelief out of obstinacy and stubbornness, which is called the unbelief of repudiation; and the other is unbelief out of ignorance and unawareness of the truth. With regard to the former, definitive rational and narrational proofs indicate that a person who deliberately and knowingly shows obstinacy towards the truth and endeavours to reject, it deserves punishment. But with regard to the latter, it must be said that if the ignorance and unawareness do not spring from negligence, they shall be forgiven and overlooked by God.

To explain this point, it is necessary to speak a bit about submission and obstinacy. The Qur'an says: "The day when neither wealth nor children will avail, except him who comes to God with a sound heart."[58]

Levels of Submission

The most basic condition of soundness of heart is to be submissive to the truth. Submission has three levels: submission of the body, submission of the intellect, and submission of the heart.

When two opponents face each other in combat and one of them feels likely to lose, he may surrender or submit to the other. In such a surrender, normally the losing opponent puts his hands up as a sign of defeat and desists from fighting, coming under the sway of his opponent. That is, he acts in accordance with whatever command his opponent gives.

In this type of submission, the body submits, but the mind and reason do not; instead, they are constantly thinking of rebellion, incessantly contemplating how to get a chance to overcome the opponent once again. This is the state of his reason and thought, and as for his feelings and emotions, they too continuously denounce the enemy. This type of submission – that of the body – is the most that can be achieved by force.

The next level of submission is the submission of the intellect and reason. The power that can make the intellect submit is that of logic and reasoning. Here, physical force can't accomplish anything. It is absolutely impossible through physical force to make a student understand that the sum of the angles of a triangle is equal to two right angles. Mathematical propositions must be proven through reasoning and not through any other way. The intellect is forced to submit through thinking and reasoning. If sufficient proof exists and is presented to the intellect and the intellect understands it, it submits, even if all the powers of the world say not to submit.

It is well-known that when Galileo was tortured for his belief in the movement of the earth and centrality of the sun in the solar system, out of fear that they would burn him alive, he expressed repentance of his scientific view; in that condition, he wrote something on the ground. It is said that he wrote, "Galileo's repentance will not make the Earth stand still."

Force can compel a person to recant his or her words, but the human intellect does not submit except when faced with logic and reasoning.

"Say, 'Produce your evidence, should you be truthful.'"[59]

The third level of submission is the submission of the heart. The reality of faith is submission of the heart; submission of the tongue or submission of the thought and intellect, if not coupled with submission of the heart, is not faith. Submission of the heart is equal to submission of the entire existence of a person and the negation of every type of obstinacy and rejection.

It is possible that someone may submit to an idea as far as the intellect and mind are concerned, but not the spirit. When a person shows obstinacy out of prejudice or refuses to yield to the truth because of personal interests, his or her mind and intellect have submitted, but the spirit is rebellious and lacks submission, and for this very reason lacks faith, since the reality of faith is the submission of the heart and soul.

God says in the Qur'an: "O you who have faith! Enter into

submission, all together, and do not follow in Satan's steps."[60]

That is, your soul should not be at war with your intellect; your feelings should not be at war with your perceptions.

The story of Satan that has come in the Qur'an is an example of unbelief of the heart, even though the intellect has submitted. Satan recognized God, believed in the Day of Judgement, completely recognized the Prophets and their legatees and admitted their position; at the same time, God calls him an unbeliever and says of him: "And he was of the unbelievers."[61]

The evidence that, in the view of the Qur'an, Satan recognized God is that the Qur'an explicitly says that he confessed that He is the Creator. Addressing God, he said: "You created me from fire, and You created him from clay."[62]

And the evidence that he believed in the Day of Judgement is that he said: "Grant me reprieve until the day they are resurrected."[63]

And the evidence that he recognized the Prophets and infallibles is that he said: "By Your might, I shall lead them all astray, except Your purified servants among them."[64]

The meaning of the purified servants, who are pure not just in their actions, but whose entire existence is purified and free of all except God, are the friends of God and the infallibles; Satan recognized them, too, and believed in their infallibility.

The Qur'an, while describing Satan as knowing all these things, calls him an unbeliever. Thus, we come to know that mere recognition and knowledge, or the submission of the intellect and mind, is not sufficient for a person to be considered a believer. Something else is necessary as well.

In the Qur'an's logic, why has Satan been regarded as an unbeliever in spite of all his knowledge?

Obviously, it is because while his perception accepted reality, his feelings rose to battle it; his heart rose against his intellect; he showed arrogance and refused to accept the truth: he lacked submission of the heart.

True Islam and Regional Islam

Normally when we say so-and-so is Muslim or isn't Muslim, our view isn't toward the reality of the matter. Those who geographically live in a particular region and are Muslims through imitation and inheritance from their parents we call Muslims; and those who live under different conditions and are affiliated with another religion or have no religion altogether, again out of imitation of their parents, we call non-Muslims.

It should be known that this aspect does not have much value, neither the aspect of being a Muslim nor that of being a non-Muslim and an unbeliever. Many of us are imitative or geographical Muslims; we are Muslims because our mothers and fathers were Muslim and we were born and raised in a region whose people are Muslim. That which has value in reality is true Islam, and that is for a person to submit to truth in the heart, having opened the door of one's heart to the truth to accept and act on it, and the Islam that he or she has accepted should be based on research and study on the one hand, and submission and lack of prejudice on the other.

If someone possesses the trait of submission to the truth and for whatever reason the reality of Islam has remained hidden from him or her without that person being at fault, God will most certainly refrain from punishing him or her; he or she shall achieve salvation from Hell. God says: "And We do not punish until We have sent a messenger."[65]

That is, it is impossible for God, the Wise and Munificent, to punish someone for whom the proofs (of truth) have not been completed. The scholars of the principles of jurisprudence have termed the purport of this verse, which acts to confirm the dictate of reason, "the improperness of punishment without prior explanation." They say that until God has made clear a reality for a person, it is unjust for Him to punish that person.

To show the fact that it is possible to find individuals who possess the spirit of submission without being Muslims in name, Descartes, the French philosopher – according to his own words – is a good example.

In his biography, they have written that he began his

philosophy from doubt; he doubted all that he knew and began from zero. He made his own thought a starting point and said, "I think, therefore I am."

After proving his own existence, he proved the spirit, and likewise the existence of body, and God became definite for him. Gradually the issue of choosing a religion arose; he chose Christianity, which was the official religion of his country.

But he also says, "I don't say that Christianity is definitely the best religion that exists in the entire world; what I say is that among the religions that I currently know and that are in my reach, Christianity is the best religion. I have no conflict with the truth; perhaps there is a religion in other parts of the world that is superior to Christianity." Incidentally, he mentions Iran as an example of a country about which he lacks information and doesn't know the religion of; he says: "What do I know? Perhaps there is a religion in Iran that is better than Christianity."

Such people cannot be called unbelievers, since they have no obstinacy; they are not deliberately seeking unbelief. They are not involved in concealing reality, which is the essence of unbelief. Such people are "dispositional Muslims." Though they cannot be called Muslim, they also cannot be termed unbelievers, since the opposition between a Muslim and an unbeliever is not like the opposition between affirmation and negation or that between the existence and non-existence of a trait in a subject capable of possessing the trait (according to the terminology of logicians and philosophers). Instead, it is the opposition of two opposites; that is, it is the opposition of two existential things, not that of one existential and one non-existential thing.

Of course, the fact that we mentioned Descartes as an example was not to depart from the basic principle we explained earlier. We stipulated from the beginning that we were not to express opinions about individuals. Our intent in mentioning Descartes as an example is that if we suppose that what he said is true and he is as submissive to the truth as his words indicate, and on the other hand truly did not have more ability to research, then he is a dispositional Muslim.

Sincerity, the Condition for the Acceptance of Actions

The second of the issues that we raised regarding the value of faith is what influence faith can have in the acceptance of actions.

Previously, in relating the proofs of those who say that the good deeds of unbelievers are acceptable to God, we said that they say that the goodness and badness of actions is related to their essence. A good deed, whether of a believer or an unbeliever, is good by its essence and must inevitably be accepted by God, since good is good no matter who does it and bad is bad no matter who does it, and since God's relation to all people is the same.

Now, we would like to add that though what has been said in the above reasoning is correct, a basic point has been neglected in it. To explain this point, we must first explain another term from the subject of the principles of jurisprudence, which is that goodness and evil are of two types: action-related, and actor-related.

Every action has two aspects, and every one of the two aspects has a separate ruling with regard to goodness or badness. It is possible for an action to be good from one dimension and not be good from the other. Similarly, the reverse is possible; and it is also possible for an action to be good or bad from both dimensions.

The two dimensions consist of the action's beneficial or harmful effect in the external world and human society, and the action's association to its doer and that person's spiritual motivations which caused that action and the goal to which the doer aspired by performing it.

From the point of view of the former, one must determine the extent of the beneficial or harmful effect of the action. And from the point of view of the latter, one must determine what type of action the doer has performed in his or her mental and spiritual framework and what goal he or she has pursued.

Human actions, in terms of the trajectory of their beneficial and harmful effects, are recorded in books of history, and history passes Judgement about them; it praises them or condemns them. But the aspect of attribution to the human soul is only recorded in the otherworldly books [of human deeds]. Books of history like great and influential actions and praise such actions; but the Divine otherworldly and celestial books, in addition to this aspect, are in search of actions that have spirit.

The Qur'an says: "Who created death and life to try you as to which of you is the best in deeds."[66]

It refers to "the best deeds," not "the most deeds," since the important thing is for us to know that when we perform an action under the influence of spiritual motives, aside from the outward appearance of the action - which is a series of movements and has its own social effects and value - spiritually we actually move in a certain direction and traverse a certain path.

The issue is not so simple as to say, "All that exists is the 'action,' the work, the muscular energy that is spent. As for the thoughts and intentions, their value lies only in preparing for the action; they are no more than a mentality and preliminary. And whatever the preliminary may be, the main thing is the action itself." To the contrary, the importance of the thought and the intention is not less than that of the action. Such a way of thinking, which maintains the primacy of action rather than the primacy of the intention and belief, is a materialistic thought. Under the names "objectivity" and "subjectivity" it gives the belief and intention behind the action no more than preliminary value. Leaving aside the fact that the invalidity of this school is clear in its own right, what is certain is that the Qur'anic teachings cannot be interpreted on the basis of such ways of thinking.

In the view of the Qur'an, our true personality and self is our spirit. With every voluntary action, the spirit moves from potentiality to actuality and acquires an effect and an attribute commensurate to its own intention and aim. These effects and habits become a part of our personality and carry us to a world appropriate to themselves from among the realms of existence.

Thus, from the first dimension the goodness and evilness of actions depends on the external effect of those actions; and from the second dimension goodness and evilness depends on the manner in which that action was performed by its doer. In the first case, our position about an action is based on its external and societal outcome; and in the second case, it is based on the internal and mental effect of the action on its doer.

If a person establishes a hospital or performs some other charitable deed with respect to the cultural, health, or economic affairs of a country, without doubt from a societal point of view and in the view of history, that action is good. That is, it is an act that benefits God's creation. In this regard, it doesn't matter what the intention was of the person who established the hospital or other philanthropic institution. Whether the intention is to show off and fulfil one's selfish instincts or whether the intention is altruistic and unselfish, from a societal point of view a charitable institution has come into being. The ruling of history with regard to people's actions is always from this aspect and in view of this particular dimension. History has no concern with people's intentions. When the masterpieces of art or architecture in Isfahān are mentioned, no one is concerned with what intention or aim the maker of the Shaykh Luṭfullāh Mosque, the Shāh Mosque, or the Thirty-Three Bridges had; history sees the outward form and calls the action a "good deed."

However, in ascertaining an action's actor-related goodness, our attention doesn't go to the societal and external effect of the action. Instead, from this aspect, we are concerned with how the action relates to its doer. In this reckoning, it is not enough for the action to be beneficial in order for it to be considered a "good deed." What counts is what the doer's intention was in performing the action, and what goal he or she wanted to attain. If the doer had a good intention and aim and performed the action with a good motive, that action is good – that is, it possesses actor-related goodness. The action itself is two-dimensional; that is, it proceeds in two dimensions: the historical and societal dimension, and the spiritual dimension. But if the doer performed the action to show off or to attract material benefit, the action is one-dimensional. It goes forward only in time and in history, and not in the spiritual dimension; and in Islamic terminology, the action does not ascend to the higher realm. In other words, in such instances, the doer has served society and raised its level but has not benefited him or herself, and may actually have committed treachery. Instead of ascending spiritually by performing the action, the doer's soul may have descended to a lower spiritual level.

Of course, our intent is not that the action-related goodness of an action is totally separate from its actor-related goodness, and that from a spiritual point of view a person should have nothing to do with actions that are beneficial to society. The intent is that a socially beneficial deed is only spiritually beneficial when the spirit, by performing that action, has travelled a spiritual path as well, having left the station of selfishness and pleasure-seeking and set foot on the station of sincerity and purity.

The relation between action-related goodness and actor-related goodness is the relation of the body to the spirit. A living being is a combination of spirit and body. Likewise, the second type of goodness must be breathed into the body of an action possessing the first type of goodness for that action to come alive.

Thus, the rational proof of the so-called intellectuals is fallacious. This proof states that "God's relationship with all His creatures is equal, and the goodness or evilness of actions is innate to them. Thus good deeds are equal for all people. And the corollary of these two equalities is that in the hereafter, the recompense of believers and unbelievers shall be the same." In this reasoning, the actions and the equality of the creatures before the Creator have been given attention; but the doer and his or her personality, aim, motive, and spiritual path – all of which necessarily cause actions to be dissimilar and cause a difference among them similar to the difference between the living and the dead – has been forgotten. They say, "What difference does it make for God whether the doer of a good deed recognizes Him or not, or is familiar with Him or not? Whether he or she performed the action for His pleasure or with some other purpose, whether the intention be seeking nearness to God or not?"

The answer is that it makes no difference to God, but it makes a difference for that person him or herself. If the person doesn't recognize God, he or she will perform one type of spiritual action and another type if he or she is familiar with God. If one doesn't know God, one's action will be one-dimensional; the action will have only action-related and historical goodness. But if one knows God, one's action will be two-dimensional and will have actor-related and spiritual goodness. If one knows God, one's action and one's self will ascend towards God, and if one doesn't know God one will not ascend. In other words, it makes no difference for God, but it does make a difference for the action. In one case, the action will be a living, ascending action, and in the other case it will be a dead, descending action.

They say that God, who is Wise and Just, will certainly not nullify the good deeds of a person on account of not having a relationship of friendship with Him.

We too believe that God will not nullify them, but we must see whether a person who doesn't recognize God actually performs a good deed that is good both in its effect and its relation to its doer, good both from the aspect of the societal order as well as from the doer's spiritual aspect. The fallacy arises because we have supposed that for an action to be beneficial to society suffices for it to be considered a "good deed." To suppose the impossible, if a person doesn't know God and yet ascends toward God through his or her action, without doubt God will not send that person back. But reality is that a person who doesn't know God doesn't break the curtain to enter the spiritual realm, doesn't traverse any of the stations of the soul, and doesn't ascend towards God's spiritual realm in order for his or her action to acquire a spiritual aspect and a form that will be a source of pleasure, felicity, and salvation for him or her. The acceptance of an action by God is nothing other than for the action to possess these qualities.

One of the primary differences between Divine laws and human laws is this very point; Divine laws are two-dimensional, and human laws are one-dimensional. Human laws have nothing to do with the spiritual order or spiritual advancement of the individual. When a government legislates taxes in the interests of the country, its goal is solely to obtain money and cover the country's expenses. The government has no concern with the intention of the taxpayer. Does he or she pay taxes freely and willingly out of love for the country and its government, or out of fear? The government's purpose is only to obtain money; even if the taxpayer curses the government under his or her breath, the government's purpose has been attained.

Similarly, when a government calls its armed forces to defend the country, it does not concern itself with the intention of the soldiers; it desires the soldiers to fight its enemies in war. It makes no difference to the government whether the soldier fights out of his free will and inclination or out of fear of the gun to his head; or whether his fighting is to show off, as a result of foolish prejudices, or in defence of truth and what is right.

However, Divine laws are not like that. In these laws, monetary dues and warriors are not wanted in absolute terms, but together with a pure intention and desire to seek nearness to God. Islam desires actions with a soul, not soulless actions. Thus, if a Muslim pays *zakāt* (Religious Tax), but with an element of showing off, it is not accepted; if he performs *jihād*, but does it in order to show off, it is not accepted. The Divine law says that a coerced soldier is useless; I want a soldier who has the soul of a soldier, who has accepted the call: "Verily God has purchased from the believers their souls and their belongings in return for Paradise"[67] and answered it sincerely.

It has been related from the Messenger of Islam in a consecutively-narrated tradition among both the Sunnis and Shī'as that he said: "The value of deeds is based on the intention." The Prophet of Islam has also said, "Every individual shall have what he or she intended." In addition, he has stated, "No deed is accepted without an intention."[68]

One tradition has been narrated in the following words: "The value of actions is in their intention, and a man shall only get that which he intended. So whoever migrated for the sake of God and His Messenger, his migration is towards God and His Messenger; and whoever migrated for the sake of worldly wealth or a woman he wished to marry, his migration is towards that thing."[69]

Imām Ja'far b. Muḥammad as-Ṣādiq, the 6th successor of Prophet Muḥammad said, "Perform your actions for the sake of God and not people, because whatever is for God, (ascends) towards God, and whatever is for the people, does not ascend towards God."

The intention is the soul of the action, and just as the body of a human being is noble because of the human soul, so too does the nobility of a human being's action depend on its soul.

What is the soul of an action? The soul of an action is sincerity. The Qur'an says: "Yet they were not commanded except to worship God, dedicating their faith to Him..."[70]

Quality or Quantity?

From the above discussion, an interesting conclusion can be obtained which is that in the reckoning of God, the value of actions is by their quality rather than their quantity. Inattention to this point has caused some people to make up fantastic stories regarding the extraordinarily valuable actions of holy personages when they see the societal dimension of those actions to be insignificant.

For example, with regard to the ring that Imām ʿAlī bestowed on a beggar while bowing in prayer, about which a verse of the Qur'an was revealed, they say that the value of that ring was equal to the revenue of greater Syria; and in order for people to believe that, they gave it the form of a tradition. In the view of these people, it was hard to believe that a great verse of Qur'an would be revealed about the bestowal of an insignificant ring. And since they were unable to believe such a thing, they created a story and raised the ring's material value. They didn't stop to think that a ring equal in value to the revenue of all of Syria would not, in the poor and indigent city of Madīnah, be found on the finger of Imām ʿAlī. Supposing such a ring was in Imām ʿAlī's possession, he would not give it to just one beggar; instead, with such a ring he would make Madīnah flourish and save all of the city's needy.

The intellect of these fantasy-weavers hasn't understood that for God a great deed has a reckoning different from material reckonings. It is as if they have supposed that the value of the ring caught God's attention and compelled Him to praise ʿAlī for the great deed he did – God be exalted from such suppositions!

I don't know what these short-sighted people have thought up regarding the pieces of bread that ʿAlī and his family bestowed in charity and about which Sūrah "Hal Ata"[71] was revealed. Perhaps they will say that the flour of that bread was not from barley, but from gold dust!

But in fact that is not the case. The importance of 'Alī and his family's action is not in the material aspect which attracts our attention; the importance of their action is that it was pure and entirely for God's sake; it was at a level of sincerity which it is beyond us even to conceive, a sincerity which was reflected in the highest realm and elicited Divine praise and glorification.

In the words of Shaykh Farīud Dīn al-'Aṭṭar: It is beyond [the power] this world to describe his spear; It is beyond that world to describe his three pieces of bread.

The importance of their action lies in what the Qur'an has quoted: "We feed you only for God's sake; we wish from you no recompense, nor any gratitude."[72]

These are the words of their heart which God, the Aware, has made known; that is, with their selflessness and sacrifice, they desired from God naught but God Himself.

The fact that the Qur'an regards the actions of unbelievers to be like a mirage, hollow and devoid of reality, is because their actions have an adorned and misleading exterior, but since they are done for lowly material and individual motives and not for God, they have no spiritual aspect.

Zubayda, the wife of the 'Abbāsid dynasty caliph Hārūn al-Rashīd, caused a river to be dug in Makkah which has been used by visitors of God's sanctuary from that time until today. This action has a very righteous exterior. The resolve of Zubayda caused this river to flow to barren Makkah from the rocky land between Ṭā'if and Makkah, and it has been close to twelve centuries that the hot, thirsty pilgrims have been making use of it.

From a worldly perspective, it is quite a great deed; but how about from the spiritual perspective? Do the Angels reckon as we do? Is their attention, like ours, drawn to the apparent magnitude of this act?

No, their reckoning is different. Using a Divine scale, they measure the other dimensions of the action. They take account of where Zubayda obtained the money for this act.

Zubayda was the wife of an oppressive and tyrannical man who had control of the public treasury of the Muslims and would do as he pleased. Zubayda had no money of her own, and she didn't spend her own wealth in this charitable act; she spent the people's money on the people.

The difference between her and other women in her position is that others would spend the public's money on their personal desires, and she spent a portion of this money on a project for the public good. Now, what was Zubayda's purpose in this action? Did she wish for her name to remain in history? Or did she truly have God's pleasure in mind? Only God knows.

It is in this reckoning that it is said that someone saw Zubayda in a dream and asked her what God gave her for the river she caused to be made. She replied that God had given the entire reward of that action to the original owners of that money.

The Mosque of Bahlūl[73]

It has been related that once a Mosque was being constructed when Bahlūl arrived and asked, "What are you doing?" They replied, "We are building a Mosque." Bahlūl asked, "What for?" They replied, "What kind of question is that? We are building it for God."

Bahlūl wanted to show the doers of that charitable work their level of sincerity. Secretly, he had a stone engraved with the words, "The Bahlūl Mosque," and at night he affixed it above the Mosque's main gate. When the builders of the Mosque came the next day and saw the sign, they became angry. They found Bahlūl and beat him for portraying the toils of others as his own work. Bahlūl retorted, "But didn't you say you built this Mosque for God? Suppose that people mistakenly think it was I who built it; God won't make such a mistake!"

How many great deeds there are which are great in our eyes, but are worthless in the eyes of God! Perhaps many great buildings, whether Mosques, mausoleums, hospitals, bridges, rest houses for travellers, or schools, have such an end; the account of such things is with God.

Belief in God and the Hereafter

The relation of this world to the hereafter is similar to the relation between the body and the spirit, or the relation of the outer aspect to the inner aspect. This world and the next are not two wholly and entirely separate worlds; this world and the hereafter together are one unit, just as a sheet of paper has two pages and a coin has two sides. This same Earth that exists in this world will appear in the hereafter in its otherworldly form. The plants and objects of this world will appear in the hereafter in their otherworldly aspect. Fundamentally, the hereafter is the celestial form of the present world.

The condition for an action to acquire a good otherworldly aspect is for it to be performed with attention to God and in order to ascend to God's higher realm. If a person doesn't believe in the hereafter and isn't attentive to God, his or her action will not have an otherworldly aspect, and thus will not ascend to the higher realm. The otherworldly aspect is the higher aspect, and the worldly aspect is the lower aspect. As long as an action does not acquire illumination and purity through intention, belief, and faith, it cannot attain to the highest realm; only an action that has a spirit can attain that station. And the spirit of an action is its otherworldly aspect.

How beautiful are the words of the Qur'an: "To Him (God) rises the pure word, and good deeds He (God) raises."[74]

This verse can be understood in two ways, and both have been mentioned in books of exegesis of the Qur'an. The first is that good deeds raise pure words and pure belief; the other is that pure words and pure belief raise good deeds and make them otherworldly. The two explanations – both of which are correct and possibly both are intended – together convey the principle that faith has an effect on the acceptance of actions and their ascent to God, and actions have an effect on the perfection of faith and on increasing the degree of faith. This principle is an accepted one in the Islamic teachings. Our reference to this verse is based on the second explanation, though as we indicated, in our view it is possible that the verse has intended both meanings at the same time.

In any case, it is a mistake for us to think that the actions of those who don't believe in God and the Day of Judgement ascend to God and acquire an otherworldly aspect.

If we are told that someone has taken the northbound highway from Tehran and continued to travel northward for several days, we will obviously not expect that person to reach Qum, Iṣfahān, or Shīrāz (which lie south of Tehran); if someone were to entertain such a possibility, we would laugh and tell him that if that person wished to go to one of those cities, he or she would have to take the southbound highway from Tehran and travel on it.

It is impossible for someone to travel towards Turkistān, yet reach the Kaʿbah.

Heaven and Hell are the two ends of a person's spiritual journey. In the next world, every person sees him or herself at his or her journey's final point; one above, and the other below; one the highest of the high, and the other the lowest of the low. "The record of the pious is indeed in *ʿIlliyīn* (the Highest Heaven)."[75] The Qurʾan also states, "The record of the vicious is indeed in *Sijjīn* (the Lowest Pit of Hell)."[76]

How is it possible for a person not to travel towards a certain destination, or to travel in a direction opposite to it, yet still reach that destination? Moving towards the highest heaven (ʿIlliyyīn) requires an intention and desire to reach it, and that in turn requires recognition and belief on the one hand, and facilitation and submission on the other. If a person has no belief in such a destination, or lacks the quality of facilitation and submission, and in short has neither any desire nor takes even the smallest step to reach it, how can one expect him or her to attain that destination? Without doubt, every path leads to its own destination, and unless God is that destination, the path does not lead to God.

The Qurʾan says: "Whoever desires this transitory life, We expedite for him therein whatever We wish, for whomever We desire. Then We appoint hell for him, to enter it, blameful and spurned. Whoever desires the Hereafter and strives for it with an endeavour worthy of it, should he be faithful—the endeavour of such will be well-appreciated."[77]

That is, if a person's level of thinking is no higher than this world and he or she has no goal higher than this world, it is impossible for that person to attain the high target of the hereafter; but Our Divine grace and benevolence demand that We grant him or her something of the worldly goal he or she desired to achieve.

There is a subtle point here: this world is the world of nature and matter; it is the world of causes and reasons. Worldly causes are in conflict with each other, and constraints also exist in this material world. Thus, for a person whose goal is this world, there is no guarantee that he or she will definitely attain that goal. The words the Qur'an has chosen to impart this point are as follows: "We expedite for him therein whatever We wish, for whomever We desire."

However, one who has a higher goal in his or her spiritual makeup has not given his or her heart to trifling goals, and who, moving forward with faith, takes steps towards a Divine object will certainly attain the goal, since God recognizes the value of good deeds; He accepts and rewards those good deeds that are presented to Him.

Here, effort and endeavour are necessary, since it is impossible for a person to move forward and attain the goal without taking a step.

Then in the next verse, the Qur'an says: "Each We assist out of the bounty of your Lord, both this group and that one; and the bounty of your Lord has not been withheld from any."[78]

That is, Our bounty is limitless; whoever sows a seed, We bring it to fruition; whoever moves towards a goal, We deliver him or her to that goal.

The Divine sages say that the Being who is necessarily existent by essence is necessarily existent from all aspects and dimensions. Thus, He is necessarily Bountiful. As a result, whoever wishes something, God assists him or her. It is not the case that if someone seeks the world, God says to him or her, "You are misguided and have acted contrary to Our guidance and direction, so We will not assist you." That is not the case; the seeker of the world is also supported and assisted by God in seeking this world and benefits from His unhesitant bounty within the limits permitted by this world of causes, mutual exclusivity, and conflicting outcomes.

In other words, this world is a place appropriate for and given to planting, growing, increasing, and harvesting. It all depends on what seed a person chooses to grow and develop and what harvest he or she wishes to reap. Whatever seed he or she chooses is exactly what will grow and develop in the rich and fertile land of this world.

True, there is an exclusive assistance particular to the people of Truth, which is called the raḥīmiyyah (exclusive) mercy; the seekers of this world are deprived of this mercy, since they do not seek it. But the raḥmāniyyah (general) mercy of God applies equally to all people and all paths. In the words of Saʿdī, the well known poet: 'The earth's surface is His all-encompassing table, From this table all partake, whether friend or foe.'

From what has been said in this discussion, a portion of the issues under examination have been resolved.

We made clear that action-related goodness is not sufficient for reward in the hereafter; actor-related goodness is also necessary. Action-related goodness is similar to a body, and actor-related goodness is similar to its spirit and life. And we explained that belief in God and the Day of Judgement is a fundamental condition of actor-related goodness. This conditionality is not based on convention, but is instead an essential and actual conditionality, just like the conditionality of a particular path with respect to reaching a particular destination.

Here, it is necessary to clarify one point, which is that some will perhaps say that actor-related goodness does not necessarily require the intention of seeking nearness to God; if a person does a good deed because of one's conscience or out of a feeling of compassion or mercy, that is sufficient for his or her action to possess actor-related goodness. In other words, a humanitarian motive is sufficient for actor-related goodness; as long as a person's motive is other than the "self", actor-related goodness is present, whether the motive be "God" or "humanism."

This point is worthy of consideration. While we don't affirm the view that it makes no difference whether one's motive be God or humanism, and we can't enter this discussion in depth right now, we do truly believe that whenever an action is performed with the motive of doing good, serving others, and for the sake of humanity, it is not the same as an action that is performed solely with selfish motives. Without doubt, God will not leave such people without any reward. Several traditions indicate that on account of their good deeds, polytheists like Ḥātim al-Ṭāʾī will not be punished or the punishment of such people will be reduced, even though they were polytheists.

We can understand this point from many traditions which we have before us.

1. ʿAllāmah[79] Majlisī quotes from the book *Thawābul Aʿmāl* of Shaykh Ṣadūq that ʿAlī b. Yaqtīn narrated from Imām Mūsā b. Jaʿfar al-Kādhim, the seventh successor of the Prophet Muḥammad that he said, "Amongst the Children of Israel there was a believer whose neighbour was an unbeliever. That unbeliever would always show kindness and good conduct towards his believing neighbour. When this unbeliever died, God made for him a house out of a type of mud which shielded him from the heat of the fire, and his sustenance would be given to him from outside his own environment, which was of fire. He was told, 'This is because of your kindness and good conduct towards your believing neighbour.'"[80]

ʿAllāmah Majlisī, after quoting this tradition, says: "This tradition and others like it are evidence that the punishment of some unbelievers in Hell will be lifted, and the verses of Qurʾan that say the punishment of the unbelievers shall not be lightened are with regard to those who have not performed such good deeds."

2. He also narrates from Imām Muḥammad b. ʿAlī al-Bāqir, the fifth successor of Prophet Muḥammad that he said, "There was a believer who lived in the land of an oppressive king. That oppressor threatened the believer, and thus, the believer fled to a non-Islamic land, arriving at the place of a polytheist man. The polytheist sat him beside himself and hosted him well. As soon as the polytheist man died, God addressed him, 'I swear by My Honour and Glory that if there were a place in Heaven for a polytheist, I would put you in that place; but O' fire, make him fear, but don't harm him.'"

Then the Imām said, "Every morning and evening his sustenance is brought for him from outside that environment." The Imām was asked, "From Heaven?" He answered, "From where God wills."[81]

3. The Noble Messenger said about ʿAbdullāh b. Judʿān who was one of the well-known unbelievers in the Age of Ignorance and one of the chiefs of Quraysh, "The one who has the lightest punishment in Hell is ʿAbdullāh b. Judʿān." He was asked why, to which he replied: "He used to give people (food) to eat."

4. In addition, the Prophet Muḥammad said with regard to several people who lived in the Age of Ignorance: "I saw in Hell the possessor of the tunic and the possessor of the cane who would drive the pilgrims, and also the woman who had a cat which she had tied up and which she would neither feed nor set free so it could find its own food. And I entered Heaven and I saw there the man who saved a dog from thirst and gave it water."[82]

Such people, who are found in more or less every age, will at least have their punishment lightened or their punishment lifted altogether.

In my view, if there are individuals who do good to other people or even to another living being – whether a human being or animal – without any expectation, not even because they see themselves mirrored in the existence of the deprived (i.e., fear that one day they may be in similar straits is not the moving factor in what they do), and instead the motive of doing good and serving others is strong enough in them that even if they know that no benefit will accrue to them and not even a single person will come to know of what they did or say so much as "God bless you" to them, yet they still do good deeds, and they are not under the influence of habit and such like, one must say that in the depths of their conscience there exists the light of recognition of God. And supposing they deny it with their tongues, they confess it in the depths of their conscience; their denial is in reality a denial of an imagined being which they have conceived in place of God, or a denial of another imagined thing which they have conceived in place of the return to God and the Day of Judgement, not a denial of the reality of God and the Resurrection.

Love of good and justice and doing good because it is good and just and worthy, without any other factor, is a sign of love of the Essence possessed of Absolute Beauty; therefore, it is not farfetched that such people actually will not be resurrected among the unbelievers, though by their tongues they are considered deniers. And God knows best.

Belief in the Prophecy and Imāmate

Now we will discuss another aspect of the issue, which is the position of those non-Muslims who are monotheists and believe in the Resurrection and perform their actions for God.

Among the People of the Book, people can be found who neither believe the Messiah (Jesus the son of Mary) nor Ezra to be the son of God; they are neither dualists nor fire-worshippers. They do not say, "The Messiah is the son of God," or "'Uzayr is the son of God," nor that Ahrāman is the god of evil; they also believe in the Day of Judgement. What is the outcome of the actions of such people?

Right now our discussion is not about those inventors, innovators, and servants of humanity who are materialists and deny God's existence, and whose practical motives naturally do not transcend the material realm. From the preceding discussions, our view regarding them from the perspective of Islam was made clear. Our discussion in this section pertains to those good-doers who believe in Creation and in the Resurrection, and thus are able to have a higher motive in their actions and work towards a goal that goes beyond the material realm.

It is said that Edison and Pasteur were such people, that they were religious people and had religious motives. That is, in their actions they, just like religious Muslims, worked for God's pleasure and with a Divine motive. In reality, these Christians (Edison and Pasteur) are not Christians [they may be called dispositional Muslims], because if they were Christians and believed in the creeds of the existing Christianity, they would regard the Messiah as God, and naturally it would not be possible for them to be true monotheists; perhaps few of today's Christian intellectuals believe in the superstitions of the Trinity.

In order to answer this question, one must determine in what way faith in the Prophethood and Imāmate are necessary, and why such faith is a condition for the acceptance of actions.

It appears that faith in the Prophets and friends of God is involved in the acceptance of actions for two reasons:

First, recognition of them goes back to recognition of God. In reality, recognition of God and His affairs is incomplete without recognition of His friends. In other words, recognition of God in a complete form is to recognize the manifestations of His guidance.

Second, recognition of the station of Prophethood and Imāmate is necessary because without it, it is not possible to obtain the complete and correct program of action to achieve guidance.

The big difference between a Muslim good-doer and an unbelieving good-doer is that the unbeliever who does good deeds does not possess the proper program to achieve guidance and thus has only a negligible chance of success. In contrast, since the Muslim has submitted to a religion that has a comprehensive and proper program for guidance, he or she is assured of success if he or she implements that program correctly.

Good deeds do not consist only of doing good to others; all obligatory, forbidden, recommended, and disliked actions also form part of the program of good deeds.

The practicing Christian, who is outside the fold of Islam and who lacks the correct program is deprived of its great gifts since he or she commits actions which are prohibited. For example, alcohol is forbidden, but he or she drinks it. We know that alcohol was prohibited because of its personal, societal, and spiritual harms and naturally one who drinks alcohol will face its harms, similar to how a person who is deprived of the guidance of a doctor may do something which makes his or her heart, liver, or nerves prematurely sick and shortens his or her life.

In the program of Islam, there are some commands which are conditional to act upon for spiritual perfection and development. It is obvious that a non-Muslim, no matter how unprejudiced and free of obstinacy, by virtue of being deprived of the complete program of human perfection, will also remain deprived of its features.

Such a person will naturally be deprived of the great acts of worship, such as the five daily prayers, fasting during the month of Ramaḍān, and pilgrimage to the House of God (Ḥajj). He or she is like someone who plants seeds without a systematic method of farming; in no way will the product such a person obtains be like that obtained by a person who sows the earth according to a comprehensive and proper program, plants at an appropriate time and weeds at the proper time, and in short performs all the necessary technical steps.

The difference between a Muslim and a non-Muslim good-doer can be explained like this: the Muslim good-doer is like a sick person who is under the care and direction of an expert doctor; his or her food and medicine are all under the direction of the doctor. With regard to the type of medicine and food and its timing and amount, he or she acts completely as directed. However, the non-Muslim good doer is like a sick person who has no such program and acts as he or she pleases; he or she eats whatever food or medicine that comes into his or her hand. Such a sick person may occasionally consume a beneficial medicine and get a positive result, but it is just as likely that he or she will make use of a medicine that is harmful or even fatal. Similarly, it is possible he or she may eat a beneficial food, but by subsequent negligence or by eating the wrong food, may cancel the beneficial effect of the first food.

With this explanation, it becomes clear that the difference between a Muslim and a non-Muslim who believes in God is that the Muslim is a theist who possesses a proper program, while the non-Muslim theist performs his or her actions without a correct program. In other words, the Muslim has been guided, and the non-Muslim, though he or she believes in God, is misguided. In this very regard the Qur'an says: "So if they submit, they will have achieved guidance."[83]

From all that we have said in the last two sections, it has become clear that all non-Muslims are not equal in terms of being rewarded for good deeds; there is a great difference between a non-Muslim who doesn't believe in God and the Resurrection and one who believes in God and in the Day of Judgement but is deprived of the gift of faith in the Prophethood. For the first group, it is not possible to perform an action acceptable to God, whereas for the second it is possible. It is possible for this group to go to Heaven under certain conditions, but for the first group it is not possible.

Apparently, the reason that Islam differentiates between polytheists and the People of the Book in its laws of interaction – in that it doesn't tolerate the polytheist but tolerates the People of the Book, it forces the polytheist to abandon his or her belief but doesn't force the People of the Book – is that the polytheist or atheist, by virtue of his or her polytheism or denial, forever closes the gate of salvation for him or herself and is in a condition of having deprived him or herself of crossing the material world and ascending to the higher world and eternal Paradise. However, the People of the Book are in a condition in which they can perform good deeds, even if in a deficient manner, and with certain conditions can attain the results of those actions.

The Qur'an says, addressing the People of the Book: "Come to a common word between us and yourselves, that we worship none but God and associate none with Him, and that we take not each other as lords in place of God."[84]

The Noble Qur'an has given the People of the Book such a call, but has absolutely not given and does not give such a call to polytheists and atheists.

Affliction

The third issue that deserves attention in relation with the value of faith is the negative value of unbelief and obstinacy. That is, do unbelief and obstinacy cause a good deed to become null and void and lose its effect, making it go bad as an affliction does? In other words, if a person performs a good deed with all the conditions of action-related and actor-related goodness, and yet on the other hand that person shows obstinacy with respect to truth, especially a truth that is one of the principles of religion, in this situation, does this deed – which in and of itself is good, otherworldly, and luminous and free of defect from the Divine and celestial dimension – become null and void because of this stubbornness and obstinacy or other devious spiritual condition? Here the question of affliction comes about.

It is possible for an action to have both action-related and actor-related goodness, and in other words to have both the proper body and a sound soul and spirit, to be good both from the worldly and from the otherworldly point of view, but at the same time to be destroyed and become null from the otherworldly point of view through affliction, just like a sound seed that is planted in fertile ground and even gives fruit, but which falls prey to an affliction before it can be used, and is destroyed, for example, by locusts or lightening. The Qur'an calls this affliction *ḥabṭ* or invalidation.

Such affliction is not exclusive to unbelievers; it can take place with respect to the good deeds of Muslims as well. It is possible that a believing Muslim may give alms to a deserving needy person for God's sake and for that deed to be accepted by God, but for him or her to later destroy that good deed and make it void by laying an obligation on the other person or some other form of mental torment.

The Qur'an says: "O you who have faith! Do not render your charities void by reproaches and affronts."[85]

Another of the afflictions of good deeds is jealousy, as has been said: "Verily envy eats away good deeds just as fire destroys wood."[86]

Another affliction is *juḥūd* or denial, or a condition of fighting with the truth. Denial means that a person perceives the truth but at the same time opposes it. In other words, denial is when one's mind has submitted through reason and logic and truth has become clear to one's intellect and power of thinking, but the spirit and its' selfish and arrogant feelings rebel and refuse to submit.

The essence of unbelief is opposition and resistance to truth while recognizing what it is. Previously, when we discussed the levels of submission, we gave some explanation regarding this condition. Here, we provide some further explanations relevant to the discussion of afflictions.

Imām 'Alī says, defining Islam: "Islam is submission."[87]

That is, when personal interest, prejudice, or habit conflicts with truth and reality, for a person to submit to truth and turn away from all that isn't truth is Islam.

Denial means a condition of wilful unbelief, the condition that Abū Jahl, one of the uncles of the Prophet Muḥammad possessed. He knew that the Noble Messenger was truthful in his claim of being a Prophet, but because he had a condition of wilful unbelief, he didn't believe in him. Sometimes people can be heard to say things like, "We're willing to go to Hell, but not to do such-and-such a thing." That is, even if that action is the truth, we still are not willing to accept it. Other expressions, such as to be a mule, to be intractable, and such like all describe this quality of denial.

The Qur'an has excellently described the presence of this quality in some people where it says: "And when they said, O' God, if this be the truth from You, rain down upon us stones from heaven, or bring us to a painful punishment."[88]

What a picture the Qur'an has painted! By narrating one sentence, it indicates the sick mentality of some people.

The obstinate person whose words have been quoted in this verse, instead of saying, "O' God, if this be the truth from You, then make my heart ready to accept it," says, "If this be the truth, send upon me a punishment and annihilate me, because I haven't the strength to remain alive and face the truth."

This condition is a very dangerous one, even if it be in small matters. And it may well be that many of us are suffering from it – God forbid!

Suppose that an eminent doctor, or *mujtahid* (Muslim Jurisprudent), or some other specialist who has a worldwide reputation makes a determination and expresses an opinion in an issue related to his or her specialization; then, some unknown, a doctor or a young student, expresses a conflicting opinion in the same issue and even presents definitive proofs which that eminent personality him or herself affirms in his or her heart the truth of what that person is saying, but other people remain unaware as they were before, and in view of the reputation of that eminent person, accept his or her view. In this situation, if that famous expert submits to the opinion of that young doctor or student, that is if he or she submits to reality and admits his or her own mistake, he or she is truly a "Muslim," because "Islam is submission," and in a way it can be said this is an example of the verse "Rather, one who submits himself to God."[89] Such a person is free of the impure trait of denial. But if he or she engages in denial and opposes the truth to save his or her standing and fame, he or she is wilfully seeking unbelief and is in a state of *juḥd* or denial.

If that doctor, for example, is not entirely unfair, he or she may not take back his or her words, but may change in practice; and if he or she is very unfair, he or she will not change in practice, either, and will give the same prescription and perhaps kill the patient, then say that the patient was beyond treatment - and the same goes for any other eminent intellectual. The opposite of this condition also occurs frequently. There is a tradition in *al-Kāfī* that sheds light on this reality.

Muḥammad b. Muslim narrated that he heard Imām Muḥammad b. ʿAlī al-Bāqir say: "Everything that results from confession and submission is faith, and everything that results from denial and rejection is unbelief."[90]

They say that the late Āyatullāh Sayyid Ḥusayn Kūhkamarī who was one of the students of the author of *Jawāhirul Kalām*[91] and a prominent and well-known *Mujtahid* and recognized teacher, would go daily at an appointed time, as was his pattern, to one of the Mosques of Najaf and teach.

As we know, the post of teaching the level of "*Khārij*" (the highest level of Islamic studies) of jurisprudence and its principles is the grounds for leadership and religious authority. Leadership and religious authority for a seminary student mean to go suddenly from zero to infinity, since a student is nothing as long as he is not a religious authority, and his opinion and belief are not given the least importance, and usually he lives a meagre life. But as soon as he becomes a religious authority, all of a sudden his view is obeyed and no one has anything to say in the face of his opinion. Financially as well as intellectually, he has full discretion without being held accountable to anyone. Thus, a scholar who has a chance of becoming a religious authority passes through a sensitive stage; the late Sayyid Ḥusayn Kūhkamarī was in such a stage.

One day he was returning from somewhere, perhaps from visiting someone, and no more than half an hour remained until his class. He thought to himself that if he were to return home in that short time, he wouldn't have time to accomplish anything, so it was better to go to the appointed place and wait for his students. He went and saw that none of his students had come yet, but he saw that in a corner of the Mosque a humble-looking Shaykh was seated and lecturing to a group of students. The late Sayyid listened to his words, and with great surprise he realized that the Shaykh's discourse was very scholarly. The next day, he was motivated to deliberately come early and listen to the words of that Shaykh. So he came and listened, and his conviction from the previous day became stronger. This was repeated for several days, and the late Sayyid Ḥusayn became sure that the Shaykh was more learned than he himself and that he could benefit from his lectures, and if his own students were to attend the Shaykh's lectures, they would benefit more.

Here it was that he saw himself as being offered a choice between submission and obstinacy, between faith and unbelief, between the hereafter and this world.

The next day when his students came and gathered, he said, "Friends, today I want to tell you something new. The Shaykh who is sitting in that corner with a few students is more deserving to teach than I am, and I myself benefit from his lectures, so let us all go together to his lecture." From that day, he joined the circle of students of that humble Shaykh who's eyes were slightly swollen and in whom the signs of poverty were visible.

This austere Shaykh was the same scholar who later became famous as Shaykh Murtaḍhā al-Anṣārī, earning the title "teacher of the latter-day scholars."

Shaykh Anṣārī at that time had just returned from a trip of several years to Mashhad, Isfahān and Kāshān and had acquired much knowledge from that trip, especially from the presence of the late Shaykh Aḥmad Narāqī in Kāshān.

Whoever this condition is found in is an example of the verse "one who submits himself to God."

Thus, unbelief and denial mean to wilfully stand in the face of the truth and show obstinacy. Later, we will mention that in the view of the Qur'an, the unbeliever has been called an unbeliever because he or she is in a state of denial and obstinacy while at the same time perceiving the truth; and it is this state that causes nullification and is considered an affliction of good deeds. This is why in relation to the actions of those who disbelieve in which they have been compared to ashes which a strong wind blows upon and destroys, God tells us:

"A parable of those who defy their Lord: their deeds are like ashes over which the wind blows hard on a tempestuous day..."[92]

Suppose that Pasteur performed his intellectual research which led to the discovery of bacteria for God and that his intention was to serve humanity and seek nearness to God, that is not sufficient for him to be rewarded by God in the end. If he possessed qualities like denial and the like and was prejudiced in favour of his own beliefs, then without doubt all his actions are null and void, since in this case he is in a state of denying the truth, and this state of opposing the truth destroys all of a person's efforts. This would be the case if, for example, it were said to him, "Christianity is a regional and an ancestral faith for you; have you researched whether there is a better and more complete religion than Christianity or not?" and he were to reject those words and – without being ready to study and search – say, "The best religion is Christianity." A person's actions, in such a case, are like ashes subject to ruin by a swift wind.

We only mentioned Pasteur as an example; we don't mean to say that Pasteur was like this. God alone knows that. If we, too, are obstinate towards to the truth, we fall into this general rule. O Lord! Protect us from the state of unbelief, obstinacy, and opposition to the truth.

Apart from what has been mentioned, there are also other afflictions that befall good deeds. Perhaps one of these afflictions is apathy and indifference in defending truth and righteousness. One must not only avoid denial and rejection of truth, but in addition, one must also not be neutral, and instead must defend the truth. The people of Kūfah (ʿIrāq) knew that truth was with Ḥusain b. ʿAlī, and they had even admitted this fact but they were neglectful in supporting and defending the truth. They didn't show resolve and perseverance. Not to support the truth is to deny the truth in practice.

Lady Zaynab, the daughter of ʿAlī, the daughter of ʿAlī, in her famous address to the people of Kūfah, rebukes them for their negligence in coming to the defence of the truth and for oppressing and sinning against it. She said: "O' people of Kūfah! O' people of deception treachery and disloyalty, do you weep? So let your tears not dry, and your cries not cease! Your parable is that of the woman who undid her weaving after having made it firm."[93]

Another of the afflictions that can befall actions is conceit and vanity. Boasting about one's deeds, like jealousy, conceit and denial, also destroys actions.

There is a tradition that says: "Sometimes a person performs a good and worthy deed, and his or her action finds a place in the *ʿIlliyyīn*, but later he or she mentions that action in public and boasts of it. This causes the action to descend. If he or she mentions it again, it descends further. When it is mentioned a third time, it is destroyed altogether, and sometimes is converted into an evil deed."

Imām Muḥammad b. ʿAlī al-Bāqir said: "Preserving a deed is harder than the deed itself." The narrator asked what preserving a deed meant. The Imām replied, "A person does a good deed and gives something in the way of God, and it is recorded for him as an act done in secret. Then he mentions it, so it is erased and recorded as an act done in public. Then he mentions it, so it is erased and recorded as an act done to show off."[94]

Below the Zero Point

So far our discussion has been of the acceptance and non-acceptance of acts of worship and good and positive deeds of non-Muslims, and in other words the above discussion was about what is above the zero point; the discussion was whether their good deeds cause them to ascend or not.

Now let us see what is the state of what is below the zero point, that is, what happens to the sins and evil deeds of non-Muslims. Are they all alike from the aspect of our discussion, or is there a difference? In addition, in these actions that are evil and bring a person down, is there a difference between Muslims and non-Muslims, and similarly between Shīʿas and non-Shīʿas? Does a Muslim, and especially a Shīʿa Muslim, have a sort of protection with regard to such actions, or not?

In the preceding matter, it became clear that God only punishes people when they commit wrong deeds out of culpability, that is, when they do so deliberately and with knowledge, not out of incapacity. Previously, we translated and explained the verse of Qurʾan from which Scholars of the principles of jurisprudence derive the rule that says "It is evil to punish one without having explained his or her duty." Now, to clarify the situation of non-Muslims with respect to actions that fall below the zero point and to study their punishment and retribution for the evil deeds they commit, we have no choice but to broach another issue that is touched upon in Islamic sciences and is rooted in the Noble Qurʾan; and that is the issue of "incapacity" and "powerlessness". Here, we begin our discussion under this heading.

The Incapable and the Powerless

The scholars of Islam make use of two terms; they say that some people are "powerless" or are "awaiting the command of God". "Powerless" refers to the unfortunate and unable; "those awaiting the command of God" denotes people whose affairs and status are to be regarded as being with God and in His hands; God Himself shall deal with them as His wisdom and mercy dictate. Both terms have been taken from the Qurʾan.

In the fourth chapter of the Qurʾan, verses 97-99, we read: "And those whose souls the Angels take while they are oppressive to themselves; they say, 'What state were you in?' They say, 'We were weak in the land.' They say, 'Was not God's earth wide, that you may migrate in it?' So the abode of those people is Hell, and evil an abode it is, except the powerless among the men, women, and children who neither have access to any means nor are guided to any way; so perhaps God may pardon them, and God is Ever-Forgiving, Ever-Pardoning."

In the first verse, mention is made of the interrogation of some people by the Divine appointees (in the grave). The Angels ask them, "What state were you in, in the world?" They forward the excuse: "We were unfortunate, our means were inadequate (and we were unable change our state)." The Angels will say, "You were not powerless, since God's earth was spacious and you could have migrated from your homeland and gone to an area where you had greater opportunity; thus you are culpable and deserving of punishment."

In the second verse, the state of some people is mentioned who are truly powerless; whether they be men, women, or children. These are people who had no means and no way out.

In the third verse, the Qur'an gives tidings and hope that God may show forgiveness towards the second group.

In his commentary of the Qur'an, *al-Mīzān*, our most esteemed teacher, ʿAllāmah Ṭabāʾṭabāʾī, has this to say regarding these very verses: "God considers ignorance of religion and every form of preventing the establishment of the signs of religion to be oppression, and Divine forgiveness does not encompass this. However, an exception has been made for the powerless who did not have the ability to move and change the environment. The exception has been mentioned in such a way that it is not exclusive to when powerlessness takes this form. Just as it is possible for the source of powerlessness to be an inability to change the environment, it is possible for it to be because a person's mind is not aware of the truth, and thus remains deprived of the truth."[95]

Many traditions have been narrated in which those people who, for various reasons have remained incapable, have been counted among the "powerless."[96]

In verse 106 of the ninth chapter of the Qur'an, God says: "And others who are awaiting the command of God, He will either punish them or He will forgive them; and God is Knowing, Wise."

The term "those awaiting God's command" has been taken from this verse.

It has been narrated that Imām Muḥammad b. ʿAlī al-Bāqir said about this verse: "Verily there was a people in the early era of Islam who were once polytheists and committed grave misdeeds; they killed Hamzah and Jaʿfar and people like them from among the Muslims. Later, they became Muslims, abandoning polytheism for monotheism, but faith did not find its way into their hearts for them to be counted among the believers and become deserving of Heaven, while at the same time they had forsaken denial and obstinacy, which was the cause of their being (deserving of) punishment. They were neither believers, nor unbelievers and deniers; these then are the *murjawn li-ʿamrillāh*, whose affair is referred to God."[97]

In another tradition[98], it has been narrated that Ḥumrān b. A'yan said, "I asked Imām Jaʿfar b. Muḥammad as-Ṣādiq about the powerless." He replied, "They are neither of the believers nor of the unbelievers; they are the ones whose affair is referred to God's command."[99]

Though the purport of the verse regarding those whose affair is referred to God's command is that one should say only that their affair is with God, still, from the tone of the verse regarding the powerless, a hint of Divine forgiveness and pardon can be deduced.

What is understood in total is that those people who in some way were incapable and are not blameworthy, will not be punished by God.

In al-Kāfī, there is a tradition from Hamzah b. Ṭayyār who narrated that Imām Jaʿfar b. Muḥammad as-Ṣādiq said: "People are of six groups, and in the end are of three groups: the party of faith, the party of unbelief, and the party of deviation. These groups come into being from God's promise and warning regarding Heaven and Hell. (That is, people are divided into these groups according to their standing with respect to these promises and warnings.) Those six groups are the believers, the unbelievers, the powerless, those referred to God's command, those who confess their sin and have mixed good deeds with evil deeds, and the people of the heights."[100]

Also in al-Kāfī, it is narrated from Zurārah that he said: "I visited

Imām Muḥammad b. ʿAlī al-Bāqir with my brother Ḥumrān, or with my other brother Bukahīr. I said to the Imām, 'We measure people with a measuring tape: Whoever is a Shīʿa like ourselves, whether among the descendants of ʿAlī or otherwise, we forge a bond of friendship with him (as a Muslim and one who will achieve salvation), and whoever is opposed to our creed, we dissociate from him (as a misguided person and one who will not achieve salvation).'"

The Imām said, "Zurārah! God's word is more truthful than yours; if what you say is correct, then what about God's words where He says, 'Except the powerless among the men, women, and children who find no way out nor find a path?' What about those who are referred to God's command? What about those regarding whom God says, 'They mixed good deeds and other, evil deeds?' What happened to the people of the heights? Who, then, are the ones whose hearts are to be inclined?"

Ḥammād, in his narration of this event from Zurārah, narrates that he said, "At this point the Imām and I began to argue. Both of us raised our voices, such that those outside the house heard us."

Jamāl b. Darrāj narrates from Zurārah in this event that the Imām said, "Zurārah! [God has made it] incumbent upon Himself that He take the misguided (not the unbelievers and deniers) to Heaven."[101]

Also in *al-Kāfī* it is narrated from Imām Mūsā b. Jaʿfar al-Kādhim that he said: "'Alī is a gate among the gates of guidance; whoever enters from this gate is a believer, and whoever exits from it is a unbeliever; and one who neither enters from it nor exits from it is among the party whose affair is referred to God."

In this tradition, the Imām clearly mentions a party who are neither among the people of faith, submission, and salvation, nor among the people of denial and annihilation.[102]

Also in *al-Kāfī*, it is narrated from Imām Jaʿfar b. Muḥammad as-Ṣādiq: "If only people, when they are ignorant, pause and don't reject, they will not be unbelievers."[103]

If one ponders upon the traditions which have come down from the pure Imāms and most of which have been collected in the sections "The Book of the Divine Proof" and "The Book of Belief and Disbelief" in al-Kāfī, he or she will realize that the Imām's position was that whatever [punishment] befalls a person is because truth was presented to him or her, and he or she showed prejudice or obstinacy towards it, or at the very least was in a position where he or she should have researched and searched, but didn't do so.

And as for people who, out of incapacity of understanding and perception, or because of other reasons, are in a position where they are not in denial or negligent in researching, they are not counted among the deniers and adversaries. They are counted among the powerless and those referred to God's command. And it is understood from the traditions that the pure Imams view many people to be of this category.

In *al-Kāfī*, in the section "The Book of the Divine Proof," Shaykh Kulaynī narrates several traditions to the effect that: "Whoever obeys God with an act of worship in which he exhausts himself, but doesn't have an Imām appointed by God, his effort is not accepted."[104]

Or that: "God does not accept the actions of His servants without recognition of him (the Imām)."[105]

At the same time, in "The Book of the Divine Proof" of *al-Kāfī* it is narrated from Imām Ja'far b. Muḥammad as-Ṣādiq: "Whoever recognizes us is a believer, and whoever denies us is an unbeliever, and whoever neither recognizes nor denies us is misguided until he or she returns to the guidance of our obedience which God enjoined upon him or her. So if he or she dies in the state of misguidedness, God shall do what He pleases."[106]

Muḥammad b. Muslim says: "I was with Imām as-Ṣādiq. I was seated to his left, and Zurārah to his right. Abū Baṣir entered and asked, "What do you say about a person who has doubts about God?" The Imam replied, "He is a unbeliever." "What do you say about a person who has doubts about the Messenger of God?" "He is an unbeliever." At this point the Imām turned towards Zurārah and said, "Verily, such a person is a unbeliever if he or she denies and shows obstinacy."[107]

Also in *al-Kāfī*, Kulaynī narrates that Hāshim b. al-Barīd (Ṣāḥib al-Barīd) said: "Muḥammad b. Muslim, Abul Khaṭṭāb, and I were together in one place. Abul Khaṭṭāb asked, "What is your belief regarding one who doesn't know the affair of Imāmate?" I said, "In my view he or she is a unbeliever." Abul Khaṭṭāb said, "As long as the evidence is not complete for him or her, he or she is not a unbeliever; if the evidence is complete and still he or she doesn't recognize it, then he or she is a unbeliever." Muḥammad b. Muslim said, "Glory be to God! If he or she doesn't recognize the Imām and doesn't show obstinacy or denial, how can he or she be considered an unbeliever? No, one who doesn't know, if he doesn't show denial, is not an unbeliever." Thus, the three of us had three opposing beliefs.

"When the Ḥajj season came, I went for Ḥajj and went to Imām as-Ṣādiq. I told him of the discussion between the three of us and asked the Imam his view. The Imām replied, "I will reply to this question when the other two are also present. I and the three of you shall meet tonight in Minā near the middle Jamarah."

"That night, the three of us went there. The Imām, leaning on a cushion, began questioning us."

"What do you say about the servants, womenfolk, and members of your own families? Do they not bear witness to the unity of God?"

I replied, "Yes."

"Do they not bear witness to the prophecy of the Messenger?"

"Yes."

"Do they recognize the *Imāmate* and *wilāyah* like yourselves?"

"No."

"So what is their position in your view?"

"My view is that whoever does not recognize the Imām is an unbeliever."

"Glory be to God! Haven't you seen the people of the streets and markets? Haven't you seen the water-bearers?"

"Yes, I have seen and I see them."

"Do they not pray? Do they not fast? Do they not perform Ḥajj? Do they not bear witness to the unity of God and the prophethood of the Messenger?"

"Yes."

"Well, do they recognize the Imām as you do?"

"No."

"So what is their condition?"

"My view is that whoever doesn't recognize the Imām is a unbeliever."

"Glory be to God! Do you not see the state of the Ka'bah and the circumambulation of these people? Don't you see how the people of Yemen cling to the curtains of the Ka'bah?"

"Yes."

"Don't they profess monotheism and believe in the Messenger? Don't they pray, fast, and perform Ḥajj?"

"Yes."

"Well, do they recognize the Imām as you do?"

"No."

"What is your belief about them?"

"In my view, whoever doesn't recognize the Imām is an unbeliever."

"Glory be to God! This belief is the belief of the Khārijites."

At that point the Imām said, "Now, do you wish me to inform you of the truth?"

Hāshim, who in the words of the late Faydh al-Kāshānī, knew that the Imām's view was in opposition to his own belief, said, "No."

The Imām said, "It is very bad for you to say something of your own accord that you have not heard from us."

Hāshim later said to the others: "I presumed that the Imām affirmed the view of Muḥammad b. Muslim and wished to bring us to his view."[108]

In *al-Kāfī*, after this tradition, Shaykh Kulaynī narrates the well-known tradition of the discussion of Zurārah with Imām Muḥammad b. 'Alī al-Bāqir in this regard, which is a detailed discussion.

In *al-Kāfī* at the end of "The Book of Belief and Disbelief," there is a chapter entitled, "No action causes harm with belief, and no action brings benefit with unbelief."[109]

But the traditions that have come under this heading do not

affirm this heading. The following tradition is among them: Ya'qūb b. Shu'ayb said, I asked Imām Ja'far b. Muḥammad as-Ṣādiq: "Does anyone aside from the believers have a definite reward from God?" He replied, "No."[110]

The purport of this tradition is that God has given a promise of reward to none but the believers, and without doubt He will fulfil His promise. However, aside from the believers, God has not given any promise for Him to have to fulfil of necessity. And since He has not given any promise, it is up to Him Himself to reward or not to reward.

With this explanation, the Imām wishes to convey that the non-Believers are counted with the powerless and those whose affair is referred to God's command in terms of whether God will reward them or not; it must be said that their affair is with God, for Him to reward or not to.

At the end of this chapter of *al-Kāfī* there are some traditions which we will mention later under the heading, "The Sins of Muslims."

Of course, the relevant traditions are not limited to those mentioned here; there are other traditions as well. Our deduction from all of these traditions is what we have mentioned above. If someone deduces something else and doesn't affirm our view, he or she may explain his or her view with its evidence, and perhaps we can benefit from it as well.

From the View of the Islamic Sages

Islamic philosophers have discussed this issue in a different way, but the conclusion they have reached in the end corresponds with what we have deduced from the verses and traditions.

Avicenna says: "People are divided into three groups in terms of soundness of body or physical beauty: one group is at the stage of perfection in soundness or beauty, another is at the extreme of ugliness or illness. Both of these groups are in a minority. The group that forms the majority are the people who in the middle in terms of health and beauty; neither are they absolutely sound or healthy, nor do they, like the deformed, suffer from deformities or permanent sickness; neither are they extremely beautiful, nor ugly."

"Similarly, from the spiritual point of view, people fall into the same categories; one group is in love with truth, and another is its stubborn enemy. The third group consists of those in the middle; and they are the majority, who are neither in love with truth like the first group, nor its enemies like the second. These are people who have not reached the truth, but if they were shown the truth, they wouldn't refuse to accept it."

In other words, from the Islamic perspective and from a jurisprudential viewpoint, they are not Muslims, but in real terms, they are Muslims. That is, they are submissive to truth and have no stubbornness toward it.

Avicenna says, after this division: "Believe God's mercy to be encompassing."[111]

In the discussions of good and evil of the philosophical text *al-Asfār*, Mullah Ṣadrā mentions this point as an objection: "How do you say that good overcomes evil even though, when we look at the human being, which is the noblest creation, we see that most people are caught in evil deeds in terms of their practice, and stuck in unsound beliefs and compound ignorance in terms of their beliefs? And evil deeds and false beliefs destroy their position on the Day of Judgement, making them worthy of perdition. Thus, the final outcome of humanity, which is the best of creation, is wretchedness and misfortune."

Mullāh Ṣadrā, in answering this objection, points to the words of Avicenna and says: "In the next life, people are the same as they are in this life in terms of their soundness and felicity. Just as the extremely sound and exceedingly beautiful, and likewise the very ill and exceptionally ugly, are a minority in this world, while the majority is in the middle and is relatively sound, so too in the next world the perfect, who in the words of the Qur'an are *al-Sābiqūn*, or "the foremost ones," and similarly the wretched, who in the words of the Qur'an are *Aṣḥāb al-Shimāl*, or "the people of the left," are few, and the majority consists of average people, whom the Qur'an calls *Aṣḥāb al-Yamīn*, or "the people of the right."

After this, Mullāh Ṣadrā says: "Thus, the people of mercy and soundness are predominant in both worlds."

One of the latter sages, perhaps the late Āqā Muḥammad Riḍā Qumshi'ī, has some unique verses of poetry about the vastness of the Lord's mercy. In these verses, he reflects the belief of the sages, and rather the broadness of the mystics' stand. He says:

Consider all to be Gods', accepted and non-accepted,
From mercy it commenced and to mercy it will return.
From mercy the created ones came, and to mercy they go,
This is the secret of love, which baffles the intellect.
All of creation was born with the innateness of Divine Unity,
This polytheism is incidental, and the incidental subsides.
Says wisdom: Keep hidden the secret of truth;
What will the prying intellect do with love, which pulls aside the curtains?
Consider the story of what was and what will be to be a dot,
This dot sometimes ascends and sometimes descends.
None but I strove to keep the trusts,
Whether you call me oppressive or call me ignorant.

The discussion of the sages pertains to the minor premise of an argument, not the major premise. The sages don't discuss what the criterion of a good deed or the criterion of a deed's acceptance are; their discussion is about the human being, about the idea that relatively speaking, in practice, the majority of people – to differing extents – are good, remain good, die good, and will be resurrected good.

What the sages wish to say is that although those who are blessed to accept the religion of Islam are in a minority, the individuals who possess innate Islam and will be resurrected with innate Islam are in a majority.

In the belief of the supporters of this view, what has come in the Qur'an about the Prophets interceding for those whose religion they approve of is in reference to the innate religion, and not the acquired religion, which, through incapacity, they haven't reached, but towards which they show no obstinacy.

The Sins of Muslims

As for the sins of Muslims, this issue has the exact opposite form of first issue (the good deeds of non-Muslims) and is the completion of the previous discussion. The issue is whether the sins committed by Muslims are similar to the sins of non-Muslims with regard to punishment or not.

Broaching the previous issue was necessary from the aspect of its being a matter of intellectual belief; but broaching this issue is a practical necessity, because one of the factors in the fall and ruin of Muslim societies in the present age is the undue pride which in the latter days has come into being in many Muslims, and also in many Shīʿas.

If these individuals are asked whether the good deeds of non-Shīʿas are acceptable to God, many of them answer, "No." And if they are asked what ruling the evil deeds and sins of Shīʿas have, they answer, "They are all forgiven."

From these two sentences, it is deduced that actions have no value; they have neither positive nor negative value. The necessary and sufficient condition for felicity and salvation is for a person to name him or herself Shīʿa, and that's it.

Normally, this group argues as follows:

First, if our sins and those of others are to be accounted for in the same way, what difference is there between Shīʿas and non-Shīʿas?

Second, there is a well-known tradition: "Love of ʿAlī is a good deed with which no evil deed can bring harm."

In answer to the first argument, it must be said that the difference between Shīʿas and non-Shīʿas becomes apparent when a Shīʿa acts on the program his or her leaders have given him or her and the non-Shīʿa also acts on the teachings of his or her own religion. In such a case, the precedence of the Shīʿa, both in this world and in the other, will become clear. That is, the difference should be sought in the positive side, not the negative side. We shouldn't say that if the Shīʿa and non-Shīʿa put the teachings of their religion under their feet, there must be some difference between them – and if there is no difference in that case, then what difference is there between Shīʿas and non-Shīʿas?

This is exactly as if two patients were to refer to a doctor, one referring to an expert doctor and the other to a doctor with less expertise, but when they receive the doctor's prescription, neither of them acts in accordance with it. Then the first patient complains, saying, "What difference is there between me and the patient who referred to the non-expert doctor? Why should I remain sick like him, even though I referred to an expert doctor and he referred to a non-expert doctor?"

Just as in the example of the two patients, it is not correct for us to differentiate between ʿAlī and others by saying that if we don't act according to his commands, we will see no harm, but for them, whether they act according to the words of their leader or not, they will be in loss.

One of the companions of Imām Jaʿfar b. Muḥammad as-Ṣādiq said to the Imām: "Some of your Shīʿas have gone astray and consider forbidden actions to be permissible, saying that religion is recognition of the Imām and no more; thus, once you have recognized the Imām, you may do whatever you want." Imām as-Ṣādiq said: "Verily we belong to God and to Him shall we return. These unbelievers have interpreted that which they don't know according to their own ideas."

The proper statement is, "Acquire recognition [of the Imām] and do whatever good deeds you want, and they will be accepted of you, for God does not accept actions without recognition."[112]

Muḥammad b. Mārid asked Imām Jaʿfar b. Muḥammad as-Ṣādiq: "Is it true that you have said, 'Once you have recognized (the Imām), do what you please'?" The Imām replied, "Yes, that is correct." He said, "Any action, even adultery, theft, or drinking wine?!" The Imām replied: "Verily we belong to God and to Him shall we return. I swear by God, they have wronged us. We [the Imāms] ourselves are responsible for our actions; how can responsibility be lifted from our Shīʿas? What I said is that once you have recognized the Imām, do what you wish of good deeds, for they will be accepted from you."[113]

As for the tradition that says: "Love of ʿAlī is a good deed with which no evil deed will cause harm," we must see what its interpretation is. One of the eminent scholars – I think it was Waḥīd Bihbahānī – has interpreted this tradition in a noteworthy way. He says that the meaning of the tradition is that if one's love of ʿAlī is true, no sin will bring harm to a person. That is, if one's love of ʿAlī - who is the perfect example of humanity, obedience, servitude, and ethics – is sincere and not out of self-centeredness, it will prevent the committing of sins; it is like a vaccine that brings immunity and keeps sickness away from the vaccinated person.

Love of a leader like ʿAlī who is the personification of good deeds and piety, causes one to love ʿAlī character; it chases the thought of sin from one's mind, with the condition, of course, that one's love be true. It is impossible for one who recognizes ʿAlī – his piety, his tearful prayers, his supplications in the heart of the night – and one who loves such a person, to act in opposition to his command, he who always commanded others to be pious and do good deeds. Every lover shows respect to the wishes of his or her beloved and respects his or her command. Obedience to the beloved is a necessary result of true love; thus it is not exclusive to ʿAlī; true love of the Prophet Muḥammad is the same way. Thus, the meaning of the tradition: "Love of ʿAlī is a good deed with which no evil deed can cause harm" is that love of ʿAlī is a good deed that prevents evil deeds from bringing harm; that is, it prevents their occurrence. It doesn't indicate the meaning that the ignorant have understood, which is that love of ʿAlī is something alongside of which any sin you may commit will not have an effect.

Some dervishes on the one hand claim to love God and on the other hand are more sinful than all other sinners; these, too are false claimants.

Imām Jaʿfar b. Muḥammad as-Ṣādiq said: You disobey God while claiming to love Him, This by my life is an incredible deed. If your love were true, you would obey Him; Verily the lover shows obedience to the beloved.

The true friends of ʿAlī would always abstain from sins; his patronage (*wilāyah*) would protect from sin, not encourage it.

Imām Muḥammad b. ʿAlī al-Bāqir said: "Our patronage is not

attained except through deeds and piety."[114]

Now, some traditions in support of this point:

1. Ṭāwūs al-Yamānī says: "I saw ʿAlī b. Ḥusain perform the circumambulation the House of God and busying himself in worship from the time of ʿIshā (night) prayers until the last part of the night. When he found himself alone, he looked toward the sky and said, "O God! The stars have disappeared in the horizon and the eyes of the people have slept, and Your gates are open to those who seek..."

Ṭāwūs narrated many sentences in this regard from the humble and worshipful supplications of the Imām and has said (in regards to the Imām): "Numerous times in the course of his supplication, he wept." He (Ṭāwūs) then said: "Then he (the Imām) fell to the earth and prostrated on the ground. I approached and, putting his head on my knees, wept. My tears flowed and fell on his face. He rose, sat, and said: "Who has busied me from the remembrance of my Lord?" I said: "I am Ṭāwūs, O son of the Messenger of God. What is this agitation and disquiet? We, who are sinners and full of shortcomings, should do thus. Your father is Ḥusain b. ʿAlī, your mother is Fāṭimah Zahrā, and your grandfather is the Messenger of God – that is, with such a noble ancestry and lofty link, why are you in discomfort and fear?"

He looked to me and said: "Not at all, O' Ṭāwūs, not at all! Leave aside talk of my ancestry. God created Heaven for those who obey Him and do good, even if he be an Abyssinian slave, and He created Hell for those who disobey him, even if he be a Qurayshī lad. Have you not heard the words of God: "So when the trumpet shall be blown, there will be no relations among them, nor shall they ask one another?" By God, nothing shall benefit you tomorrow except what good deeds you send forth."[115]

2. The Messenger of God, after the conquest of Makkah, ascended the hill of al-Ṣafā and called out: "O sons of Hāshim! O sons of ʿAbdul Muṭṭalib!" The descendents of Hāshim and ʿAbdul Muṭṭalib assembled; when they came together, the Messenger addressed them: "Verily I am God's Messenger to you; verily I am your well-wisher. Don't say that Muḥammad is from among us, for I swear by God, my friends from among you and from among others are only

the pious ones. So do not let me see you come to me on the Day of Judgement carrying the world on your shoulders, while the people come carrying the Hereafter. Aye, I have left no excuse between myself and you, and between God the Exalted and you. Verily, for me are my deeds and for you are your deeds."[116]

3. Books of history have written that the Noble Messenger, in the last days of his life, went out alone at night to the cemetery of al-Baqīʿ and sought forgiveness for those buried in it. After that, he said to his companions, "Each year Jibrāʾīl would show the Qurʾan to me once, and this year he recited it for me twice. I think this is a sign that my death has approached." The next day he went to the pulpit and declared, "The time of my death has approached. Whoever I have made a promise to, let him come forward so that I may fulfil it, and whoever is owed something by me, let him come forward so that I may give it."

Then he continued his words thus: "O people! Verily there is no kinship between God and any person, nor is there anything on account of which He will do good to a person or cast away evil from him except deeds. Aye, let no one claim or wish (otherwise). I swear by Him Who sent me with the truth, nothing will give salvation save (good) deeds along with mercy, and if [even] I were to disobey, I would perish. O God! I have conveyed."[117]

4. Imām ʿAlī b. Mūsā al-Riḍā had a brother known as Zayd al-Nār. The character of this brother of the Imām was not very pleasing to the Imām. One day, during the time that the Imām was in Marw, Zayd was present in a gathering in which there was a large group of people who were speaking to each other. While the Imām was speaking, he noticed that Zayd was talking to a group of people and speaking of the station of the Messenger's family, and in a proud manner would constantly say, "we this" and "we that." The Imām cut short his own words and said, addressing Zayd: "What are these things that you are saying? If what you say is correct and the descendents of the Messenger of God have an exceptional status; that is, if God is not to punish their evildoers and will reward them without their doing good deeds, then you are more honourable near God than your father Mūsā b. Jaʿfar, because he would worship God

until he attained the stations of Divine proximity, whereas you think that without worship you can attain the station of Mūsā b. Jaʿfar."

The Imām then turned to Ḥasan b. Mūsā al-Washshāʿ, one of the scholars of Kūfah who was present in that gathering, saying, "How do the scholars of Kūfah recite this verse: "O Noah! Verily he is not of your family; he is a (doer) of unworthy deeds."

He replied: "They recite it thus: "That is, he is not your son and is not from your seed; he is the son of an unrighteous man."

The Imām said, "Such is not the case. They recite the verse incorrectly and interpret it incorrectly. The verse is thus: That is, your son himself is unworthy. He was actually the son of Noah; he was driven away from God and drowned because he himself was unrighteous, even though he was the son of Prophet Noah.

Thus, being descended from and related to the Prophet or Imām has no benefit; good deeds are required."[118]

Creational Conditions and Conventional Conditions

Usually, people compare the Divine rules in creation, reward and punishment, and salvation and perdition to the human societal rules, even though these affairs are in accordance with creational and actual conditions and are a portion of them, whereas social conditions and rules follow conventional, man-made rules. Social rules can follow conventional conditions, but the rules of creation, and among them Divine reward and punishment, cannot follow these conditions, and instead follow creational conditions. To clarify the difference between a creational system and a conventional system, we present an example:

We know that in social systems, every country has its own particular rules and laws. Social rules, in some issues, differentiate between two people who are equal in physical and creational conditions, but different with respect to conventional conditions.

For example, when they wish to hire someone in Iran, if an Iranian and an Afghani apply for the job and both are equal in terms of creational conditions, it is possible that the Iranian will be hired rather than the Afghani, simply because he is not an Iranian. In this case, if the Afghani says that I am completely equal in terms of physical conditions to the Iranian who was hired – if he is healthy, I too am healthy, if he is young, so am I, if he is a specialist in such-and-such a field, so am I – he will be given the answer that administrative rules do not permit us to hire you.

Based on a conventional and man-made decision, the position of this same Afghani individual can change and become like others; that is, he can apply for and receive Iranian citizenship. It is obvious that citizenship papers have no effect on his actual personality; but from the view of social rules, he has become another person. Normally, the observance of conventional conditions is concurrent with a lack of observance of equality in actual and creational conditions.

But in issues that do not follow social and conventional rules and instead follow only creational conditions, the case is different.

For example, if – God forbid – an illness or an epidemic comes to Iran, it will not differentiate between a citizen of Iran and that of another country. If an Iranian and an Afghani are equal with respect to temperamental, environmental, and all other conditions, it is impossible for the bacteria that cause illness to discriminate and say that since the Afghani is not a citizen of Iran, I have nothing to do with him. Here, the issue is of creation and nature, not society and societal conventions; the issue pertains to creation, not to legislation and rule-making.

The Divine rules with respect to reward and punishment and salvation and perdition of individuals are subject to actual and creational conditions. It is not the case that if someone claims, "Since my name is recorded in the register of Islam and I am Muslim by name, I must have special treatment," it will be accepted of him or her.

Let there be no confusion; here we are concerned with the discussion of reward and punishment, salvation and perdition, and the conduct of God with His servants; we are not talking about the laws that Islam has legislated in the Muslims' social life.

There is no doubt that the laws of Islam, like all other legislations of the world, are a series of conventional laws, and a series of conventional conditions has been observed within them. And in these laws which are related to their worldly life, human beings, out of necessity, must follow a set of conventional conditions.

But the actions of God, and the operation of Divine will in the system of creation – including the granting of salvation and leading to perdition of individuals and rewarding and punishing them – do not follow social rules, and instead are of another type altogether. God, in carrying out His absolute will, does not act on the basis of conventional rules. Conventional matters which naturally have a major effect on social systems have no role in the creational will of God.

From the viewpoint of the rules which Islam has legislated that pertain to the social conduct of human beings, whenever a person recites the two testimonies[119], he or she will be recognized as a Muslim and will benefit from the advantages of Islam. But with regard to the rules of the hereafter and from the viewpoint of God's conduct, the laws of: "Whoever follows me, is from me..."[120] and: "Verily the most honourable of you near God is the most pious of you."[121]

The Messenger of God said: "O people! Verily your father is one, and your Lord is One. All of you are from Adam, and Adam was from dust. There is no pride for an Arab over a non-Arab, except through piety."[122]

Salmān al-Fārisī, who strove to reach truth, reached such a station that the Noble Messenger said of him, "Salmān is one of us, the People of the House."

There are some who have come under the influence of satanic whisperings and have contented themselves with the thought: "Our name is among the names of ʿAlī friends. However we may be, we are considered his subjects. Or we will make a will that a large sum out of the money that we have acquired through wrong means or that we should have spent in our lifetime in good causes – but didn't – should be given to the caretakers of one of the holy shrines in order for us to be buried near the graves of God's saints, so that the Angels don't dare punish us."

Such people should know that they have been blinded and the curtain of negligence has covered their eyes. Their eyes will open when they will find themselves drowned in Divine punishment and they will suffer from such regret that if it were possible to die, they would do so a thousand times. So let them awake from the slumber of carelessness today, repent, and make up for what has passed.

"And warn them (of) the day of regret, when the affair will be decided while they are negligent and don't believe."[123]

From the point of view of the Qur'an and the Islamic traditions, it is definite that the sinner, even if Muslim, will be punished by God. True, since he or she has faith, he or she will in the end achieve salvation and liberty from Hell, but it may be that this salvation will only come after years of hardship and punishment.

Some people's account of sins will be cleansed by the hardships of dying; another group will pay the penalty for their sins in the grave and *barzakh* (intermediary realm between this world and the next); another group will get their retribution in the horrors of Resurrection and difficulties of accounting for their deeds; and yet others will go to Hell and linger there for years in punishment. It has been narrated from the sixth Imām, Ja'far b. Muḥammad as-Ṣādiq that the verse: "...lingering therein for ages..."[124] pertains to those who will attain salvation from Hell.[125]

Here we mention some examples of traditions which talk of the punishments of the time of death and after death so that they may help us take notice, awaken, and prepare ourselves for the daunting and dangerous stations which we have ahead of us.

1. Shaykh Kulaynī narrates from Imām Ja'far b. Muḥammad as-Ṣādiq that 'Alī was once suffering from pain in the eye. The Prophet Muḥammad went to visit him at a time when he was crying out from the pain. He said, "Is this cry from impatience, or because of the severity of pain?" 'Alī replied, "O Messenger of God, I have not suffered any pain like this until today." The Prophet began to narrate the terrifying account of what happens to unbelievers when they die. Upon hearing this, 'Alī sat up and said, "Messenger of God, please repeat this account for me, for it made me forget my pain." Then he said, "O Messenger of God! Will anyone from your

community face such a death?" He replied, "Yes: a ruler who oppresses, one who usurps the property of an orphan, and one who bears false witness."[126]

2. Shaykh Ṣadūq narrates in the book *Man Lā Yahdhrul Faqih* (For the Person who does not have a Jurisprudent at Hand) that when Dharr, the son of Abū Dharr al-Ghifārī, died, Abu Dharr stood by his grave, put his hand on the grave, and said: "God have mercy on you; I swear by God that you were good to me and now that you have left me I am pleased with you. I swear by God that I am not worried because of your leaving; nothing has been diminished from me, and I am in need of none but God. And were it not for the fear of the time of notification, I would wish that I had gone in your place. But now I wish to compensate for what has passed and prepare for the next world, and verily my grief for your sake has prevented my grief over you. [That is, I am absorbed in thinking about doing something that could benefit you, and so I have no time to grieve at being separated from you.] I swear by God that I have not wept on account of your separation, but I have cried thinking about how you are and what you have gone through. I wish I knew what you said and what was said to you! O God! I have forgiven the rights that You had made obligatory on my son for me, so You too forgive him Your rights over him, for magnanimity and generosity are more befitting of You."[127]

3. Imām Ja'far b. Muḥammad as-Ṣādiq narrates from his noble ancestors that the Prophet Muḥammad said, "The squeezing in the grave for a believer is an atonement for the shortcomings he or she has committed."[128]

4. 'Alī b. Ibrāhīm narrates from Imām Ja'far b. Muḥammad as-Ṣādiq regarding the verse: *"...and beyond them is a barrier until the day they shall be resurrected."*[129] that he said: "I swear by God, I fear nothing for you except *barzakh*; as for when the affair is committed to us, we are more worthy of you."[130]

That is, our intercession is related to after *barzakh*; there is no intercession in *barzakh*.

In general, there are so many Qur'anic verses and clear traditions regarding the punishment for sins such as lying, backbiting, false accusation, treachery, oppression, usurping other's property, drinking, gambling, tale-bearing, defaming, abandoning prayer, abandoning fasting, abandoning pilgrimage, abandoning *Jihād*, and so forth that it is beyond reckoning; none of them are exclusive to the unbelievers or non-Shīʿas. In the tradition of the *Miʿrāj* (Prophetic ascent to Heaven), we find many examples where the Prophet Muḥammad says: "I saw various groups of my community, men and women, in different forms of punishment, who were being punished on account of various sins."

Summary and Conclusion

From all that has been said in this section about the good and bad deeds of Muslims and non-Muslims, the following conclusions can be reached:

1. Both salvation and perdition have degrees and levels; neither the people of salvation are all at the same level, nor are those of perdition. These levels and differences are called *darajāt* "levels of ascent" with regard to the people of Heaven and *darakāt* "levels of descent" with regard to the inhabitants of Hell.

2. It is not the case that all of the dwellers of Heaven will go to Heaven from the beginning, just as all of the people of Hell will not be in Hell for eternity. Many dwellers of Heaven will only go to Heaven after suffering very difficult periods of punishment in *barzakh* or the hereafter. A Muslim and a Shīʿa should know that, assuming he or she dies with sound faith, if God forbid he or she has committed sins, injustices, and crimes, he or she has very difficult stages ahead, and some sins have yet greater danger and may cause one to remain eternally in Hell.

3. Individuals who don't believe in God and the hereafter naturally don't perform any actions with the intention of ascending towards God, and since they don't perform good deeds with this intent, by necessity they do not embark on a journey towards God and the hereafter. Thus, they naturally don't ascend towards God and the higher realm and don't reach Heaven. That is, because they were not moving towards it, they don't reach that destination.

4. If individuals believe in God and the hereafter, perform actions with the intention of seeking nearness to God, and are sincere in their actions, their actions are acceptable to God and they deserve their reward and Heaven, whether they are Muslims or non-Muslims.

5. Non-Muslims who believe in God and the hereafter and do good deeds with the intention of seeking nearness to God, on account of being without the blessing of Islam, are naturally deprived of benefiting from this Divine program. That proportion of their good deeds is accepted which is in accordance with the Divine program, such as forms of favours and services to God's creation. But invented acts of worship that without base are naturally unacceptable, and a series of deprivations resulting from unavailability of the complete program apply to and include them.

6. Accepted good deeds, whether of Muslims or otherwise, have certain afflictions which may come about afterwards and corrupt them. At the head of all of these afflictions is rejection, obstinacy, and deliberate unbelief. Thus, if non-Muslim individuals perform a great amount of good deeds with the intention of seeking nearness to God, but when the truths of Islam are presented to them show bias and obstinacy and set aside fairness and truth-seeking, all of those good deeds are null and void, "like ashes caught in a strong wind on a stormy day."

7. Muslims and all other true monotheists, if they commit indecencies and transgressions and betray the practical aspect of the Divine program, are deserving of long punishments in *barzakh* and the Day of Judgement, and occasionally because of some sins, like intentionally murdering an innocent believer, may remain in eternal punishment.

8. The good deeds of individuals who don't believe in God and the Day of Judgement and perhaps may ascribe partners to God will cause their punishment to be lessened and, occasionally, be lifted.

9. Felicity and perdition are in accordance with actual and creational conditions, not conventional and man-made conditions.

10. The verses and traditions that indicate that God accepts good deeds do not look solely to the action-related goodness of

actions; in Islam's view, an action becomes good and worthy when it possesses goodness from two aspects: action-related, and actor-related.

11. The verses and traditions that indicate that the actions of those who deny Prophethood or the *Imāmate* are not acceptable are with a view to denial out of obstinacy and bias; however, denial that is merely a lack of confession out of incapacity - rather than out of culpability - is not what the verses and traditions are about. In the view of the Qur'an, such deniers are considered *mustaḍ'af* (powerless) and *murjawn li'amrillāh* (those whose affair is referred to God's command).

12. In the view of the Islamic sages such as Avicenna and Mullāh Ṣadrā, the majority of people who haven't confessed to the truth are incapable and excusable rather than culpable; if such people do not know God they will not be punished - though they will also not go to Heaven - and if they believe in God and the Resurrection and perform pure good deeds with the intention of seeking nearness to God, they will receive the recompense for their good deeds. Only those will face perdition who are culpable, not those who are incapable.

"God! Seal (our fate) for us with goodness and felicity, and cause us to die as Muslims, and join us with the righteous, Muḥammad and his noble Progeny (may peace be upon all of them)."

Glossary of Terms

Ahlul Bait: The select members of the family of the Prophet Muhammad. They hold a special place in Islam, having been mentioned in the Noble Qur'an in chapter 33, verse 33 in which Allāh has confirmed that they are spiritually pure and infallible. Along with the Qur'an, all Muslims are obligated to follow the code of conduct of the Prophet Muhammad and his family – the Ahlul Bait.

Ahlul Kitāb: Lit. 'The People of the Book'. This is an honorific title mentioned in the Qur'an and the Prophetic tradition in regards to the Jews and Christians – those who were given a Divine Book from Allāh. This title is also extended to the Sabians and the Zoroastrians

Allāh: The proper name of God used by Muslims and even non-Muslim Arabic speakers.

Āyatullāh: Lit. the 'Sign of Allāh'. This is an honorific title given to scholars of the highest calibre who, after years of study, are worthy of being followed and taken as guides on the path.

Barzakh: This is the Arabic word for the period of life after death in which the soul of the deceased is transferred across the boundaries of the mortal realm into the spirit world and into a kind of "cold sleep" where the soul will rest until the Judgement Day. It is a term referred to in Islamic eschatology and the Qur'an. Barzakh is a sequence that happens after death, in which the archangel Azrael or his helper angels will separate the soul from the body, either harshfully or painlessly depending on how righteous the person was before his death. Three events make up Barzakh: The separation of the soul and the body; Nakir and Munkar's interrogation of the soul; Finally, the "Waahsh" or the horror of the grave, the pressure of the grave depending on whether the person was righteous or not. The soul rests in peace or torment until Judgement Day, based on whether the soul answered the three questions correctly or falsely.

Faqīh: Lit. 'Jurisprudent.' A scholar of Islāmic law who has reached to the status of being able (and permitted) to elucidate upon the Islāmic injunctions found in the corpus of Islāmic legal tradition.

Ḥajj – One of the fundamental acts of Islām which each and every Muslim, male or female, is obliged to perform at least once in his/her lifetime if the requirements are fulfilled.

Imām – Lit. 'leader.' This word has a general and specific meaning attached to it. The general meaning is any guide or scholar who leads the community in acts of worship and other areas. The specific meaning of this word is restricted to the 12 infallible leaders which came after the death of the Prophet Muḥammad and were Divinely appointed by Allāh to lead the Muslim nation.

Imāmate: The belief in the guidance of the 12 infallible leaders who came after the death of the Prophet Muḥammad.

Jihād: Lit. 'to struggle.' This word, which has been misused in the recent past, carries many definitions with it including a war fought to preserve the Islāmic lands, the religion Islām and the Muslims. However, its initial meaning and that which is seen in the Noble Qur'an is its literal meaning which is to strive and struggle in various walks of life. The Qur'an refers to the spending of wealth to promote goodness as being a "Jihād", just as it refers to protecting the downtrodden and oppressed people as a form of "Jihād".

Khārijites: Lit. 'Those who split off or depart.' The name of a reactionary 'Islāmic' group that emerged during the fighting between Imām 'Ali and the Umayyad Dynasty founder who tried to establish his own caliphate to enforce his own personal gains and interests.

Madressah: Lit. 'A place to learn.' The common application of this word is any form of school – whether it be a state run school such as kindergarten, primary, secondary schools which impart 'secular' knowledge, or even religious schools which run on a weekly basis (such as a Sunday school) or a full-time Islāmic theological seminary.

Miʿrāj: Lit. 'The Night Ascension.' This is in reference to the miraculous night journey of the Prophet Muḥammad which took place in the city of Mecca in which he journeyed to Jerusalem and then into the heavens to witness the greatness of the world of creation. The Qur'an refers to this event in atleast two passages – chapter 17, verse 1 and chapter 53, verses 1 to 18.

Mujtahid: The status or title one arrives to after having completed his Islāmic studies in Jurisprudence after which he would be given the authority to extract the Islāmic legal rulings from the Qur'an and the Traditions of the Prophet and the Ahlul Bait.

Murjī': The Murjī' appeared on the Islāmic arena during Umayyad era. They played a dangerous role in formulating the political events at those times and had supported and defended the Umayyad government.

Qur'an: Lit. "The Recitation", it is the holy book of Islām. Muslims believe that the Qur'an is the literal word of God and the culmination of God's revelation to mankind, revealed to the Prophet Muhammad over a period of 23 years through the Angel Gabriel.

Quraysh: Refers to the Meccan tribe that Muhammad belonged to. Ironically, it was his own tribe that was his chief opponent for most of his life.

Ramaḍhān: The ninth month of the lunar calendar, it is the month in which the Qur'an was revealed to the Prophet Muḥammad and in which all Muslims over the age of maturity are obligated to fast from the break of dawn until the end of the day.

Sayyid: An honorific title given to those who are the blood relations to the Prophet Muḥammad through the clan of Banī Hāshim.

Shīʿa: Lit. 'a follower.' The Shīʿa, which make up roughly 25% of the total Muslim population of the world today with large concentrations in Iran, Iraq, Pakistan, India, Bahrain, Syria, Lebanon, North America and Europe follow the Noble Qur'an and the way of the Prophet Muhammad. However, based on the directive of the Prophet in following his Ahlul Bait (family), the Shīʿa also follow Imam ʿAlī and the eleven successors which come from his progeny. It is a misnomer to claim that the Shīʿa do not follow the 'Sunnah' of the Prophet Muḥammad as this is a required aspect of faith in Islām which the Qur'an itself testifies to. Rather, the Shīʿa follow the Sunnah as conveyed to them through the legitimate channel of conveyance of the knowledge – his pure and immaculate family members.

Shaykh: Lit. 'an elder.' This word is customarily used as an honorific title for a scholar due to his wisdom and sagacity which normally is seen in older people.

Taqlīd: Lit. 'to follow.' This is a term which refers to the laity following the scholars of the faith in order to fulfil their religious responsibility to Allāh.

Tawhīd: Lit. 'monotheism.' This is the cornerstone upon which the faith of Islām is built. The main belief of the Muslims is that Allāh (God) is one – He has no partners, children, spouse, etc... to help or share in His Authority.

Wilāyat: This word means means power, authority or a right of certain kind. In Shīʿa theology, 'wilāyat' is the authority invested in the Prophet and the Ahlul Bayt as representatives of Almighty Allāh on this earth.

Zakāt – A general ʿArabic term which refers to 'purification', its legal definition in the Islamic legislation refers to a specific 'tax' levied on Muslims. The amount of this 'tax' differs according to various circumstances and the detailed rules of this obligatory act can be found in the works of Islāmic jurisprudence.

Notes

1 *The Noble Qur'an*, 2:253, which states: "We have made some of these messengers to excel the others among them are they to whom Allāh spoke, and some of them He exalted by (many degrees of) rank; and We gave clear miracles to Jesus son of Mary and strengthened him with the holy spirit. And if Allāh had pleased, those after them would not have fought one with another after clear arguments had come to them, but they disagreed; so there were some of them who believed and others who denied; and if Allāh had pleased they would not have fought one with another, but Allāh brings about what He intends." Also, 17:55 which reads: "And your Lord best knows those who are in the heavens and the earth; and certainly We have made some of the prophets to excel others, and to David We gave a scripture." **[Please note that the first number denotes the chapter, while the second number is the verse.]**

2 *The Noble Qur'an*, 33:7 which states: "And when We made a covenant with the prophets and with you, and with Noah and Abraham and Moses and Jesus, son of Mary, and We made with them a strong covenant." Also see *The Noble Qur'an*, 42:13: "He has made plain to you the religion that He enjoined upon Noah, and that which We have revealed to you, and that We have enjoined upon Abraham, Moses, and Jesus..."

3 *The Noble Qur'an*, 3:84

4 It took the Catholic Church almost two thousand years to recognize the non-Christians including the Muslims. The Second Vatican Council declared in 1964 that "Those who, through no fault of their own, do not know the Gospel of Christ or his church, but who seek God with a sincere heart, and moved by grace, try in their actions to do his will as they know it through the dictates of their conscience–those too may achieve eternal salvation." *Vatican Council II: The Conciliar and Post Conciliar Documents* (Wilmington, Delaware: Scholarly Resources, 1975) pg. 367.

5 The fourth in a chain of twelve Divinely appointed successors to the Prophet Muḥammad.

6 Imām ʿAlī Zaīnul ʿĀbidīn, *Risālatul Ḥuqūq*, tr. SSA Rizvi (Vancouver: VIEF, 1989) pg. 36.

7 Ira Lapidus writes: "The Ottomans, like previous Muslim regimes, considered the non-Muslim subjects autonomous but dependent peoples whose internal social, religious, and communal life was regulated by their own religious organizations, but their leaders were appointed by, and responsible to, a Muslim state." *A History of Islamic Societies* (NY: Cambridge

University Press, 1990) pg. 323. Also see Marshall Hodgson, *The Venture of Islam*, vol. 1 (Chicago: University of Chicago Press, 1974) pg. 306.

8 Ira Lapidus, *A History of Islamic Societies* (NY: Cambridge University Press, 1990) p. 323. Also see Marshall Hodgson, *The Venture of Islam*, vol. 1 (Chicago: University of Chicago Press, 1974) p. 306.

9 Hick, *God and the Universe of Faith* (London: Macmillan, 1977) pg. 140.

10 Hick, *An Interpretation of Religion* (New Haven: Yale University Press, 1989) pp. 364-365.

11 John Hick, *An Interpretation of Religion*, p. 241. In other words, we cannot really know God; what we know is our perception of Him. Muslim philosophers do not accept Kant's theory. For more on the theory of knowledge from the Islamic perspective in English, see Sayyid Muḥammad Ḥusayn Ṭabā'ṭabā'ī, *The Elements of Islamic Metaphysic*, tr. S.A.Q. Qarā'i (London: ICAS Press, 2003) pp. 115-132 and also Part One of S.M. Bāqir as-Ṣadr, *Our Philosophy*, tr. Shams C. Inati (London: Muḥammadi Trust, 1987).

12 *The Essential Rumi*, translated by C. Barks (New Jersey: Castle Books, 1997) pg. 525.

13 *The Noble Qur'an*, 2:257

14 See the discussion in this book. Āyatullāh Muṭahharī's comment that "the reality of submission has a particular form in each age" is also key to the proper understanding of *The Noble Qur'an*, 2:62.

15 *The Noble Qur'an*, 3:19

16 *The Noble Qur'an*, 3:19-20

17 Muḥammad Ibrāhīm Āyatī, *Tārīkh-e Payghambar-e Islam* (Tehran: Tehran University Press, n.d.) pp. 480-482.

18 Ibid, pp. 483-494.

19 *The Noble Qur'an*, 31:15

20 This sketch of the life and works of Āyatullāh Muṭahharī is based chiefly on Muḥammad Wa'izzāda Khurāsānī's, *Sayrī dar Zindagi-yi 'Ilmī wa Inqilābīyi Ustad Shahīd Murtadhā Muṭahharī*, in *Yadnāma-yi Ustād Shahīd Murtadhā Muṭahharī*, ed. 'Abdul Karīm Surūsh, Tehran, 1360 Sh./1981, pp. 319-380, an article rich in information on many aspects of the recent history of Islamic Irān. Reference has also been made to Mujtabā Muṭahhari, *Zindagi-yi Pidaram*, in Harakat (journal of the students at the Tehran Faculty of Theology), no. 1 (n.d.), pp. 5-16; M. Hoda, In Memory of Martyr Muṭahharī, a pamphlet published by the Ministry of Islamic Guidance, Tehran, April, 1982;

and Āyatullāh Muṭahharī's autobiographical introduction to the eighth edition of *'Ilal-i Girayish ba Maddīgarī*, Qum, 1357 Sh./1978, pp. 7ff.

21 *'Ilal-e-Girayish ba Maddīgarī*, pg. 9.

22 Muṭahharī's name comes ninth in a list of clerical detainees prepared by the military prosecutor's office in June, 1963. See facsimile of the list in Dihnavi, Qiyam-e-Khunin-i 15 Khurdad 42 ba Rivāyat-e-Asnād, Tehran, 1360 Sh./1981, pg. 77.

23 Text of Āyatullāh Khumaynī's eulogy in *Yādnama-yi Ustād-i Shahīd Murtadha Muṭahharī*, pp. 3-5.

24 The belief of the Shi'a Muslims is that before passing away, the Prophet Muḥammad appointed (through the directive of Allāh), twelve individuals who would succeed him. This chain of successors continued from the day of the death of the Prophet and continues until the end of the world. The twelfth of these successors, according to the Shi'a belief, went into occultation and will re-appear along side Prophet Jesus to establish the kingdom of God upon the Earth. (Ed.)

25 A famous Shi'ī scholar who had produced numerous works, some of which are still taught in the traditional seminaries, thus, earning him a high rank in the traditional scholarship. He left this world in 1281 AH/1864 CE. (Ed.)

26 A famous Shi'a scholar who passed away in 637 AH/1239 CE. He has left behind countless works which Muslims of today refer to and follow. (Ed.)

27 A famous Shi'a scholar who has left behind countless works which Muslims of today refer to and follow. (Ed.)

28 A descendent of the Prophet Muḥammad buried in the city of Ray, Iran. (Ed.)

29 A descendent of the Prophet Muḥammad and sister of the 8th Divinely appointed Imām of the Shi'a tradition, 'Alī ibne Mūsā al-Riḍā. (Ed.)

30 The son of 'Ali, the first Imām of the Shi'a tradition and nephew of Prophet Muḥammad. (Ed.)

31 The son of the nephew of Prophet Muḥammad. (Ed.)

32 A companion of the Prophet Muḥammad. (Ed.)

33 *Usd al-Ghāba*, under 'Uthmān ibn Maz'ūn

34 *The Noble Qur'an*, 46:9

35 The objection may come to mind that the purport of this verse is contrary to what is accepted by Muslims as established fact, meaning that the Prophet was informed of his praiseworthy place on the Day of Judgement and of his

intercession for various sinners, and is rather contrary to the purport of various verses, like "And verily your Lord will grant you until you are pleased" (*The Noble Qur'an*, 93:5) and "For God to forgive that which has passed of your mistake and that which is to come." (*The Noble Qur'an*, 49:2)

The answer is that the purport of the verse, as is also understood from the preceding tradition, is that the end result of a person's actions are not known with certainty by anyone; only God has certain knowledge of the final result, and if others come to know, it is only by Divine revelation. So the verse that negates knowledge of the final end relates to the Prophet Muḥammad or someone else making a forecast relying on his or her own actions; and the verses that indicate that the Prophet Muḥammad has knowledge of his own or other people's final end are through Divine revelation.

36 *Biḥārul Anwār*, vol. 3, pg. 165

37 George Jordac's words about the Prophet Muḥammad indicate he believed in his prophecy and receiving Divine revelation, and he also believed firmly that ʿAlī was a man of God and regarded him as being like Jesus, but at the same time he did not abandon Christianity. Gibrān Khalīl Gibrān says of ʿAlī "In my view, ʿAlī was the first Arab to have contact with and converse with the universal soul [of the world]."

He expresses greater love for ʿAlī than even the Prophet Muḥammad. He has unusual statements about ʿAlī; for example, he says: "He died while prayer was between his two lips."

And he also says of ʿAlī, "ʿAlī was before his time, and I don't know the secret of why destiny sometimes brings people to the world before their time."

Incidentally, this point is the meaning of one of ʿAlī's own statements; he says: "Tomorrow you will see my days and my secrets will be exposed to you, and you will know me after my space has become empty and others take my place."

38 *The Noble Qur'an*, 2:256

39 *The Noble Qur'an*, 3:85

40 Of course, this does not mean that all things have the same relation to God and deserve the same treatment. The relation of things to God is not the same, but the relation of God to things is the same. God is equally close to all things, but things are different in their closeness and distance from God. There is an interesting sentence in one of the supplications read during the month of Ramaḍhān in this regard: In this sentence, God has been described thus: "Who is distant and thus cannot be seen, and Who is near and thus witnesses all conversations."

In fact, it is we who are far from Him, while He is close to us. This is an enigma; how is it possible for two things to have a different relation with each other in terms of closeness and distance? But yes, such is the case here; God is close to things, but things are not close to God – that is, they have varying states of closeness and distance.

The interesting point in this sentence is that when it describes God as being "far," it mentions an attribute of His creations as evidence, which is the attribute of sight: "None can see Him." And when it describes God as being "near," it mentions an attribute of God as evidence, which is the attribute of Divine presence and awareness. When speaking of our state, we use the attribute of "distance" for God, and when speaking of His state, we use the attribute of "closeness." Saʿdī says:

"He is a Friend closer to me than myself, and amazing it is that I am far from Him. What to do; who can I tell that the Friend is by my side, and I am forsaken!"

41 *The Noble Qur'an*, 2:80-82

42 *The Noble Qur'an*, 3:24-25

43 *The Noble Qur'an*, 2:111-112

44 *The Noble Qur'an*, 4:123-124

45 *The Noble Qur'an*, 99:7-8

46 *The Noble Qur'an*, 9:120

47 *The Noble Qur'an*, 18:30

48 *The Noble Qur'an*, 5:69

49 *The Noble Qur'an*, 14:18

50 *The Noble Qur'an*, 24:39

51 Ibid.

52 *Al-Kāfī* is one of the prime books of reference for the Shīʿa Muslims and contains traditions (the sayings and related actions) of the Prophet Muḥammad and his twelve appointed successors. (Ed.)

53 *Wasāʾilush Shīʿa* is another prime reference book for the Shīʿa Muslims. (Ed.)

54 *Mustadrak al-Wasāʾil* is another reference book for the Shīʿa Muslims. (Ed.)

55 The largest reference text of the Shīʿa Muslims which has been compiled in 110 volumes. (Ed.)

56 The 5th Divinely appointed leader after the death of the Prophet Muḥammad.

57 *Wasā'ilush Shī'a*, vol. 1, Part 1, pg. 90

58 *The Noble Qur'an*, 26:88-89

59 *The Noble Qur'an*, 27:64

60 *The Noble Qur'an*, 2:208

61 Ibid., Verse 34

62 *The Noble Qur'an*, 7:12

63 Ibid., Verse 14

64 *The Noble Qur'an*, 38:82-83

65 *The Noble Qur'an*, 17:15

66 *The Noble Qur'an*, 67:2

67 *The Noble Qur'an*, 9:111

68 This and the previous two traditions are in *Wasā'ilush Shī'a*, vol. 1, pg. 8

69 *Ṣaḥīh al-Muslim*, vol. 6, pg. 48

70 *The Noble Qur'an*, 98:5

71 *The Noble Qur'an*, Chapter 76

72 *The Noble Qur'an*, 76:9

73 Bahlūl was a companion and disciple of the 6th Shi'a Imām who was forced to pretend that he was mental unstable to avoid being executed. Anecdotes of his life are well known throughout the Muslim community and are commonly quoted as a basis of learning important lessons from.

74 *The Noble Qur'an*, 35:10

75 *The Noble Qur'an*, 83:18

76 Ibid., Verse 7

77 *The Noble Qur'an*, 17:18-19

78 Ibid., Verse 20

79 An honorific title given to Muslim scholars of the highest ranking.

80 *Biḥārul Anwār*, vol. 3, pg. 377 (Kumpānī print)

81 Ibid., vol. 3, pg. 382, (Kumpānī print), from *Al-Kāfī*

82 Both this and the previous tradition are in *Biḥārul Anwār*, vol. 3, pg. 382, (Kumpānī print), as recorded from *Al-Kāfī.*

83 *The Noble Qur'an*, 3:20

84 Ibid., Verse 64

85 *The Noble Qur'an*, 2:264

86 *Biḥārul Anwār*, vol. 15, Part 3, pg. 132-133 (Ākhūndī print)

87 *Nahjul Balāgha*, Saying 125

88 *The Noble Qur'an*, 8:32

89 *The Noble Qur'an*, 2:112

90 *Al-Kāfī*, vol. 2, pg. 387

91 This work is one of the most renowned and comprehensive compendiums of Shi'a Islāmic Jurisprudence compiled in the 18th Century.

92 *The Noble Qur'an*, 14:18

93 *Nafas al-Mahmūm*, pg. 393

94 *Wasā'ilush Shī'a*, vol. 1, pg. 55

95 *al-Mīzān*, vol. 5, pg. 51

96 Ibid., vol. 5, pg. 56-61, "Discussion of the Traditions"

97 Ibid., vol. 9, pg. 406, from *al-Kāfī*

98 A tradition is report of the sayings and reported actions of the Prophet Muḥammad and one of his twelve Divinely designated successors which form the basis of law for the Muslims alongside the Noble Qur'an. (Ed.)

99 Ibid., vol. 9, pg. 407, from *Tafsīr al-'Ayyāshī*

100 *al-Kāfī*, vol. 2, "Kitab al-Īmān wa al-Kufr," section "A'nāf al-Nās," pg. 381 (Ākhūndī print)

101 Ibid., pg. 382

102 Ibid., pg. 388

103 Ibid.

104 Ibid., vol. 1, pg. 183

105 Ibid., pg. 203

106 Ibid., pg. 187

107 Ibid., pg. 399

108 Ibid., vol. 2, chapter on deviation (Dhalāl), pg. 401

109 Ibid., vol. 2, pg. 463

110 Ibid., vol. 2, pg. 464

111 *al-Ishārāt*, towards the end of the seventh section (nama).

112 *Mustadrak al-Wasā'il*, vol. 1, pg. 24

113 *al-Kāfī*, vol. 2, pg. 464

114 *Biḥārul Anwār*, vol. 12 (Kumpānī print)

115 Ibid., vol. 11, pg. 25, "Chapter on the Noble Morals of the Fourth Imām"

116 *Biḥārul Anwār* (Ākhūndī print), vol. 21, pg. 111, from Attributes of the Shī'a by Shaykh Ṣadūq.

117 *Commentary of Nahjul Balāgha* by Ibne Abil Ḥadīd, vol. 2, pg. 863

118 *Biḥārul Anwār* (old print), vol. 10, pg. 65

119 Meaning that the person bears witness that there is no creature or entity worthy of worship except for Allāh and that Muḥammad is His Prophet and Messenger. (Tr.)

120 *The Noble Qur'an*, 14:36

121 *The Noble Qur'an*, 49:13

122 *Tārīkh al-Ya'qūbī*, vol. 2, pg. 110

123 *The Noble Qur'an*, 19:39

124 *The Noble Qur'an*, 78:23

125 *Biḥārul Anwār* (Kumpānī print), vol. 3, pg. 376-7

126 Shaykh 'Abbās Qummī ﷺ, *Manāzilul Ākhirah* (Islamiyya print), pg. 5-6

127 Ibid., pg. 24-25

128 *Biḥārul Anwār* (Kumpānī print), vol. 3, pg. 153, from *Thawābul A'māl* and *al-Amālī* of Shaykh Ṣadūq

129 *The Noble Qur'an*, 23:100

130 *Biḥārul Anwār* (Kumpānī print), vol. 3, pg. 151, from Tafsīr 'Alī b. Ibrāhīm

Do you have any questions on this book or the faith of Islam in general? Would you like a free copy of the English Translation of the Noble Qur'an? For this and any other information on Islam and the Muslims, please feel free to call or write:

Academy for Learning Islam
Box 12 150-11331 Coppersmith Way
Richmond, BC, Canada, V7A 5J9
Tel: 604-214-0786 · Fax: 604-648-8370
www.academyofislam.com
director@academyofislam.com

Islamic Humanitarian Service
81 Hollinger Crescent
Kitchener, Ontario, Canada, N2K 2Y8
Tel: 519-576-7111 · Fax: 519-576-8378
www.al-haqq.com
ihs@primus.ca

Darul Tabligh North America
786 Summa Avenue
Westbury, NY, USA, 11590
Tel: 516-334-2479 · Fax: 516-334-2624
www.darultabligh.org
info@darultabligh.org

www.ingramcontent.com/pod-product-compliance
Lightning Source LLC
Chambersburg PA
CBHW030306100526
44590CB00012B/537
* 9 7 8 1 8 9 8 4 4 9 8 3 6 *